NO MORE CHEEKS TO TURN?

NO MORE CHEEKS TO TURN?

by
Sunday Bobai Agang

HIPPOBOOKS

Copyright © 2017 by Sunday Bobai Agang

Published 2017 by HippoBooks, an imprint of ACTS, Langham Publications, WordAlive and Zondervan.

Africa Christian Textbooks (ACTS), TCNN, PMB 2020, Bukuru 930008, Plateau State, Nigeria. **www.africachristiantextbooks.com**

Langham Creative Projects, PO Box 296, Carlisle, Cumbria, CA3 9WZ, UK. **www.langhamcreative.org**

WordAlive Publishers, PO Box 4547, GP0-00100 Nairobi, Kenya **www.wordalivepublishers.com**

Zondervan, *3900 Sparks Dr. SE, Grand Rapids, Michigan 49546.* **www.zondervan.com**

ISBN: 978-9966-003-38-6

Cover design: **projectluz.com**

Book design: To a Tee Ltd, **www.2at.com**

16 17 18 19 20 /DHV/ 20 19 18 17 16 15 14 13 12 11 10 9 8 7 6 5 4 3 2 1

To the praise of our God, Creator, Redeemer, Father and Lord and to the victims of violent persecution

CONTENTS

ACKNOWLEDGEMENTS

My interest in the study of violence and how it affects humanity dates back to the 1980s. My birthplace, Kafanchan in Kaduna State, Nigeria, used to be the place from which violence spread to other parts of the northern region. Growing up there, I never imagined that I would eventually develop a passion for the study of the subject and how it informs, shapes and determines the theology of the Christian community.

This book had its beginnings in a West African Christian Writers Workshop organized by the Overseas Council International in February 2010 and led by Isobel Stevenson and Bill and Joan Houston. By the end of that workshop, I had developed a proposal for a popular book on violence, which I hoped to finish within a year. But after finishing the first draft, I became discouraged and abandoned the manuscript. Then in 2011, Donna Maxfield asked to see the manuscript and gave me helpful feedback. My thanks go to her for her encouragement and for her willingness to edit the several drafts that I sent to her. I am also grateful to Rev. Dr Ron Rice, who read the entire manuscript and made some invaluable recommendations for improvement. Mrs. Isobel Stevenson had given me similar observations. I sincerely thank her for taking time to read through the manuscript and make suggestions about how to bring the study to a level that will help pastors and church members who are struggling with the challenge of conflict violence in Africa. Dr Paul Todd, my former lecturer in Nigeria, also encouraged me to write. I thank him for his invaluable advice.

I would also like to thank Archbishop Kwashi and Dr Craig Keener for graciously providing a foreword to this book, and the Revd Gideon Para-Mallam for allowing us to use his editorial which reminds us that

Christians in Kenya and in other parts of Africa are wrestling with the same issues we face in Nigeria.

Finally, my wife, Sarah and our children, Nancy, Esther, Kent and Dorcas, have stood by me during the writing of this work. Thank you for having been there for me.

FOREWORD
BY ARCHBISHOP KWASHI

Sadly, violence and terrorism are facts of life in many countries of the world today. The causes and roots of such situations are not simple, and neither are the responses of a Christian.

Basing his work and his examples on his own country of Nigeria, the author shows how entrenched attitudes and inherited judgements play a negative role in conflicts. Christians should not look to God in order to find support for their predetermined views and to justify their actions. We need to study the Scriptures carefully, being aware of the context, and trying to discern what God is saying to his people in the situation today.

The author has himself experienced at first hand the violence, killing, pain and suffering inflicted by one group upon another, and so he deals with emotional and retaliatory responses with sympathy and understanding, but also with a firm thoroughness as he expounds the Scriptures.

Written in a simple and engaging style, but based on thorough research and scholarship, the book challenges all Christians to a way of life that will be more truly Christ-like. Working for peace and reconciliation will never be easy, but this is our calling, and because of his incomparable power, the God who calls us is indeed able to "transform our situation of desperation and agitation into a situation of hope".

In 1987 more than one hundred churches and several Christian homes and businesses were destroyed by Muslim arsonists in Zaria. They carried out this evil without government intervention of any sort until the deed was done. As the chairman of the local CAN (Christian Association of Nigeria) at that time, I circulated all churches and Christians throughout Zaria asking them not to retaliate, and miraculously the Christians stood still and watched the destruction of their property during the 72 hours of arson.

While terrorism, violence and persecution of Christians will not go on forever, the Christ-like life we live will last for eternity. Our response therefore in trying and testing times such as those Bobai describes in Northern Nigeria is a test of our faith, and we must not fail.

It is my pleasure to recommend this book most highly not only to individual Christians but also to churches and community groups. It will repay careful consideration and study, and by the grace of God, can become a powerful tool in the much needed transformation of society today.

The Most Rev Dr Benjamin A. Kwashi
Anglican Archbishop of Jos

FOREWORD
BY CRAIG KEENER

Some years ago peaceful, unarmed Christians protesting against the imposition of sharia law were gunned down in the Nigerian city of Kaduna. Sunday Agang, who was my student at the time, was anxious about the safety of his wife and brothers, whom he thought might have been present during the protest. We later learned that they were safe, but Sunday still had good reason to feel devastated.

As Sunday and I prayed together, I evoked the biblical cries of the oppressed. "Rise up, O Lord, mighty warrior!" I cried. "Trample down the enemies of your people!" When I finished, Sunday prayed. "Oh God, forgive them!" he pleaded. "We know where we will be when we die, but our oppressors have no hope." Sunday loved his enemies and prayed for those who persecuted him. I, however, was embarrassed. My prayer was biblical, but Sunday's followed an even purer biblical path, and I was moved by his example.

"Blessed are the peacemakers," Jesus said. That blessing certainly includes Sunday. In this book, Sunday deals sensitively with feelings and experiences that he understands all too well, feelings of fear, mourning, frustration, and anger. In the end, however, he still summons us to follow the costly way of our Lord Jesus. He invites us to recount stories of hope, rather than stories that incite more violence. As James warns us, "Let everyone be quick to hear, slow to speak, slow to anger, since human anger does not effect God's righteousness" (Jas 1:19–20). Working for peace can be difficult and costly, as the martyrdoms of Gandhi, King, and especially our Lord Jesus remind us. But Jesus modelled the way of peace, and invites us to be his disciples even when it is difficult.

Our specific responses to others' hatred may vary depending on the situation, but love, forgiveness, and, wherever possible, working for peace remain key expressions of faithfulness to our Lord's teachings. Working for peace does not mean inaction in the face of genocide. It also does not mean naïve trust or the assumption that our enemies will always become our friends. Sometimes trust must be earned, as in the case of Joseph's brothers. Joseph was initially readier to forgive than to trust, probably a wise impulse on his part given what he had experienced before. But the ideal remains Romans 12:17–21: Never seek vengeance; whenever possible, live peacefully with all; always leave vengeance to God, and seek to overcome evil by doing good. Indeed, sometimes, when one pleases the Lord, the Lord makes even our enemies to be at peace with us (Prov 16:7).

Craig Keener
Asbury Theological Seminary, Kentucky

1

LIVING IN DARKNESS AND THE SHADOW OF DEATH

We look for justice, but find none; for deliverance, but it is far away.

— Isaiah 59:11

We live on a continent that God has blessed with rich resources, but one that is also racked by violence of all kinds – interpersonal, interethnic, inter-religious and socioeconomic. These days, the sky is further clouded by Islamist extremism, which has inflicted extreme violence in countries like Sudan, Kenya, Mali, Congo, Cameroon, the Central African Republic, and Somalia. It can truly be said that the majority of Africans live in social darkness and in the shadow of political and economic death.

African Christians live in the same reality as everyone else, and Africa's violent crises have deeply affected them. Some are on the brink of despair. I know of a pastor whose church was burnt and several of its members killed by Boko Haram Islamists. His people are no longer willing to listen to sermons on turning the other cheek. Instead, they are asking him to keep guns in the church to ward off the next Muslim attack.

I have heard of an evangelical seminary where several students and alumni have lost their lives in religious violence. Students and lecturers are struggling to grasp what Jesus meant by "turn the other cheek". They are asking: "Does this apply only to individuals? How do we react as a group?" Some even argue that Christians in Nigeria are experiencing war, and that they are thus entitled to arm themselves as combatants fighting what they regard as a "just war".

I also know many widows whose husbands were killed. They too are saying that they have turned the second cheek and have no more cheeks to turn.

I am writing as one whose knowledge of the effects of violence is also deeply personal. I was nine years old when the Biafran War broke out in 1967. I can still remember the horrors of that time and the loss of thousands of people from all regions of Nigeria.

I have also lost many friends and relations in the violence in Kaduna and elsewhere, and I live with the memory of losing those I loved. I vividly recall learning of the death of Rev. Tacio Dunio, whom the Muslims hacked to death in Kaduna in 1987. He was a vibrant leader whom God had used to stabilize Christ's church in Kaduna. He had risen to the position of vice-president of ECWA, one of the largest denominations in Nigeria. At his memorial service I did not want to hear any message about not revenging his death. I was already a pastor but I wanted to hear our community elders calling on the youth to go and fight the Muslims.

I remember the death of my neighbour, Bobai Tokan, in the Kafanchan religious violence of 1992. Then there was my cousin, Rev. Ishaya Bobai Aniya, who was killed in the sharia violence of 2001, along with other colleagues of mine. I was in the United States studying for my Master's degree and was arranging for him to join me. We had been going to share a house and study together.

I also remember Oji, a student at JETS, the ECWA seminary in Jos, who was killed in the Boko Haram violence in Maiduguri. Daniel Shem was another vibrant student finishing his theological studies at JETS when he fell victim to the violence in Jos in 2010.

I mention these deaths to make it clear that I have lived through much of the violence in Nigeria. This book is the product of my reflection on it and the larger African experience of conflict. My prayer is that this book will help African Christians overcome their fear of suffering and death and become radical disciples of Jesus Christ. May they be led on the same journey as I was, so that they too may move from a fierce desire for revenge to being able to pray for those who have killed their loved ones. May we all learn to pray that God will forgive our enemies and grant them grace to repent.

Study Questions

1. Do you know what it is to live in darkness and the shadow of death?
2. Have those around you ever experienced that?
3. Can you tell others in the group about your experience?

2

THE SOURCES OF VIOLENCE IN AFRICA

What has gone wrong? Why have so many Africans been denied the privilege of enjoying peace and unity? We cannot respond wisely to violence if we do not know what causes it.

In looking for the answers to these questions, I have read books by those who study such things and have found that much of what they say is backed up by my own experience growing up in Nigeria. This combination of theory and life has helped me to understand what is happening and has shaped my response to it.

As you read what follows, think about how it matches your own experience.

Our History

European colonialism had a devastating impact on Africa. You can see this simply by looking at a map of Africa. The neat lines that mark the borders of different countries did not arise on their own, nor were they negotiated over centuries as happened in Europe. Instead, these are artificial boundaries created by colonial rulers during the so-called Scramble for Africa that took place between 1881 and 1914. Africa regained its independence in the 1960s and 1970s, but those brief years of colonial rule threw many different ethnic groups together in new nations that lacked the ability to accommodate such cultural and ethnic diversity. Political independence thus opened the floodgates of identity conflict and ethnic competition.

I saw this first-hand as I was growing up.

I was born into the small Moro'a ethnic group in 1958, two years before Nigeria was granted independence. The new country of Nigeria included more than three hundred ethnic groups, each with its own language, traditions and cultures. Cracks began to show barely two years after independence.

The Biafran War broke out when I was only nine and living in Kafanchan, a town in what is now Kaduna State. Kafanchan was a railway junction and thus a melting pot for the different tribes in Nigeria. You could say that, in its own way, the railway brought the tribes together by connecting the different regions of Nigeria and supporting a thriving trade network. Many Igbos came from the east and settled in Kafanchan. I can remember my father giving them land to farm so that they could eat. For the most part, we lived more or less peacefully, united by our common hatred and fear of the dominant groups in Kaduna, the Hausa-Fulani tribes.

On 15 January 1966, Nigeria experienced its first coup, which was led by two Igbo army men and resulted in the assassination of many of Nigeria's leaders. In our region, resentment grew. It was widely claimed that the majority of those who died were Northerners. Igbo communities in northern Nigeria came under violent attack. Thousands were massacred and about a million Easterners fled, convinced that they would be safer in their traditional homeland than elsewhere in the federation of Nigeria.

The refugees included people to whom my father had given farmland. They no longer felt safe in Kafanchan. By May, Igbo businesses and homes were being burnt and there were open calls for them to go back where they came from. I remember people from my village, including some of my cousins, joining in the looting of Igbo homes and shops.

Soon there were calls for the Eastern Region to separate. Attempts to salvage the federation met with no success. On 26 May 1967, the Eastern Region voted to secede from Nigeria. On 30 May, Chukwuemeka Odumegwu Ojukwu, the Eastern Region's military governor, announced the establishment of the Republic of Biafra. The colonial boundaries had broken down and Nigeria was officially at war.

The factors that led to this war are similar to those operating in many other countries in Africa. The Congo, for example, gained its independence from Belgium in the 1960s and immediately fell into long series of ethnic and regional wars. It has never been effectively reunited. Portugal's former colonies of Angola and Mozambique also slipped into ethnic civil wars after independence, as did Britain's former colony Sudan.

The cultural, religious and ethnic diversity of Africa should have been seen as a special gift from the Creator, to be used to benefit all. Instead elites have used these differences to prop up their own power by pitting African peoples against each other, impeding internal development in general and political progress in particular.

Our Stereotypes

African society is communal and so great stress is laid on the family and on the ethnic and religious group to which one's family belongs. This determines who is "in" and who is "out", who is an equal and who is not. While this communal approach to life brings many blessings, it also means that we tend to rely heavily on stereotypes.

As a young Moro'a boy I did not pay much attention to ethnic tension. I knew the fundamentals: The Igbo were money-grabbing and the Yoruba were gregarious, ostentatious and uncouth. The Hausa-Fulani were not to be trusted because they wanted to enslave the whole of northern Nigeria and forcibly convert us to Islam. As for the smaller ethnic/tribal groups: They were small, just like my tribe, so there was some level of trust between us. Call it strength in numbers.

Of course, most of us knew enough to take these stereotypes with a very large pinch of salt. Except, of course, that the stereotype of the Hausa-Fulani was rooted in historical reality. Usman dan Fodio (1754–1817) had conquered the smaller ethnic groups, forcibly converted them to Islam and established slave caliphates all over the region. This historical fact, coupled with other events in Nigerian history, had convinced northern tribes that "no good ever comes out of trusting those Hausas-Fulani. All they want to do is subjugate and humiliate."

As the tension built up over the months preceding the Biafran War, I could see that the myths and stereotypes that we had about other ethnic groups were somehow becoming magnified. A rumour spread that the Igbos were digging holes in their homes, covering the holes with mats and then inviting Moro'a women into the house. There they would fall into a hole and die. It was nonsense, but such myths fuelled suspicion between the tribes.

While such stereotypes may seem harmless, they become excuses to see people in other groups as threatening. Just as the Igbo were seen as a threat in Nigeria, so other groups are stigmatized elsewhere in Africa. These misconceptions about who belongs and who does not are responsible for the ongoing lack of assimilation, national unity and sense of national security and stability in many African countries.

Our Stories

African parents love to tell their children stories about the heroes of the past. This is the way much of our history has been preserved over the centuries. It is also a way to teach morals and ethics. Parents tell stories about heroes vanquishing wicked tribal groups, hoping that the children will grow up to become famous warriors like their ancestors. Thus children learn that the way to become famous is to wage war. These stories are often linked with religious beliefs and practices.

In Nigeria, for example, Fulani children are told how their Muslim kinsmen in West Africa raided and conquered villages and towns in countries like Ghana, Cameroon and Niger. They learn about the Fulani warlord Usman dan Fodio, who fought and conquered most of Hausaland and part of the Middle Belt. They are told that Usman dan Fodio was brave because all Fulanis are brave. These stories take root in fertile soil and sprout to produce ongoing attacks on the Plateau State and in southern Kaduna State. Non-Hausa children, of course, hear these stories told from a different perspective, and learn to hate and fear the Hausa.

We need to remember that storytelling has real consequences. The stories we have heard affect how we respond to violence against us and to any real or perceived threat.

Our Politics

Politics in itself is not evil. It is the way in which individuals and groups participate in making meaningful contributions to their communities and the greater society. Ideally, politics should focus on ensuring that all citizens enjoy free exercise of their human rights and achieve their God-given potential through the wise use of national and natural resources.

Unfortunately, in much of Africa, politics has not focused on promoting the interests of all and creating a true sense of national unity. Minority ethnic groups have been ignored. Politicians focus more on gaining power for their own group than on serving the nation. Fearing that their time in power will be limited, they seek to accumulate as much personal wealth as possible. This situation has widened the gap between rich and poor and largely destroyed the middle class.

This style of politics has resulted in ongoing political instability so that our nations have actually moved away from – rather than towards – the actualization of their vast potential. That is why even a relatively successful African state like Côte d'Ivoire was split by a civil war between its mostly Muslim north and its primarily Christian and African Traditionalist south. When it was hit by economic problems in the 1980s and 1990s, its people turned to their ethnic, religious and regional communities for protection rather than to a state they did not trust to defend them.[1]

Similarly, during the 1950s as Nigeria prepared for independence from the British, smaller groups feared being dominated by the larger groups, specifically the Hausa, Igbo and Yoruba. These larger groups also feared each other and watched jealously for any sign that another group was getting more than its fair share. Thus large conflicts arose in relation to the censuses conducted in 1962 and 1963. The higher the population of a region, the more resources it was assigned from the federal budget. Accusations were hurled that census data was being manipulated to favour particular groups. Predictably, this all descended into farce, with politicians blaming and counter-suing each other under

---

[1] Daniel Chirot, *Contentious Identities: Ethnic, Religious, and Nationalist Conflicts in Today's World* (New York: Routledge, 2011), p. 18.

the guise of safeguarding their own ethnic groups' interest – although the only interests the politicians were safeguarding were their own.

It was this type of dispute playing on ethnic insecurity that led to millions of deaths in the Biafran War. I watched young soldiers march through Kafanchan, singing as they went to board the trains that would take them to war and hardship. They were young men in the prime of life, seduced into a war not of their own making by wily politicians who masked their greed by exploiting ethnic fears. And I too believed the lies that I was being told. I too believed that we needed to act in solidarity with the president because he was one of "us", not one of "them".

If I'd known then what I know now, I would have wanted to give some of those young men a slap on the cheek to wake them up to what was being done to them! They were being sent to unbelievable hardship and death.

Politicians in Nigeria still like to play one group off against another. This too was a skill in which the colonial governments in Africa excelled, and it has borne bitter fruit.

Our Resources

Africa is rich in natural resources such as oil, gold, diamonds and other minerals. Those who can control access to these resources will be wealthy. Accordingly individuals and ethnic groups are prepared to use every available means to get access to what they regard as their share of "the national cake". One of the factors contributing to the zeal with which the Biafran War was fought was the fact that oil had been discovered in the territory claimed as Biafra. Similarly, in the late 1980s Angola was torn apart as factions supported by multinational corporations and other governments fought to control resources such as diamonds and offshore oil.

Those who control the supply of natural sources do not use it to benefit others. Thus despite Nigeria's huge oil revenues, the majority of Nigerians are very poor and have no prospect of getting a job. The oil revenue is misappropriated by a few and used for their own benefit. Why are we surprised that there is tension between northern and southern Nigeria when poverty in the north is three times what it is in the south, and no steps are being taken to address the problem? No wonder groups like Boko Haram appeal to desperate people.

Politicians do not mention economic motives in their speeches. They talk about the need to fight injustice, particularly religious and political injustice, but their fine talk is often intended to conceal the fact that their main concern is their own interests. Unfortunately, many of those listening to them fail to see the motives that underlie what is being said.

But we should not heap too much blame on politicians alone, for they too are often manipulated by powerful international forces that are happy to wage proxy wars to advance their own economic and political interests, regardless of what happens to the people of a country far away.

Our Ethics

In African Traditional Religion, fear of the wrath of evil spirits, fear of the ancestors and fear of sorcery restrained people's natural inclination to sin. The coming of the gospel and the message of God's grace and forgiveness freed us from that fear, but unfortunately many Christians have not replaced it with the biblical virtues that keep a Christian faithful, honest and true in all transactions. Many who claim to be religious show by their actions that they neither fear God nor care about their fellow human beings. They do not know how to integrate their private morality with their public life.

Many politicians, too, separate politics from morality on the assumption that the public space is a no go area for God – although they may pretend to be devout and moral if this will win them votes. Once elected to leadership they pass laws that give them immunity from the rule of law.

Striving for wealth and power by any means possible comes naturally to politicians the world over. But when Western politicians are corrupt and steal from the public purse or accept kickbacks or commit sexual sin, they are likely to go to prison or at least not be re-elected. Not so in Africa. Here politics is identified with the public display of power, popularity and wealth, and people are happy to give standing ovations to corrupt politicians. The common attitude seems to be "I'd do the same if I had the chance." Nigerians re-elect politicians who have embezzled millions. Many Liberians still supported Charles Taylor despite the atrocities his forces committed in Liberia and Sierra Leone. How do we explain such a disregard for the morality of our politicians? Is it a hangover from the days when tribal chiefs had undisputed access to wealth and power? Disgust with such attitudes has led many talented Nigerians to emigrate to foreign countries. They have little desire to return to a land where they may be kidnapped and held for ransom or murdered outright.

There is also no longer any insistence from the public that promises should be kept. Politicians and other leaders conveniently forget what they promised as soon as they have achieved their goal. They put policies in place to benefit themselves and feel free to flout the law, knowing that they can get away with it. The masses know this very well, and so when emotions run high they take the law into their own hands. This is the only way they know to get justice. But with no independent arbitrator, such actions often set off a chain of reactions that lead to the destruction of lives and property.

Nigeria's founding fathers envisaged an independent Nigeria as a country where every Nigerian would have the opportunity to participate as a dignified human being in the economic and political development and scientific progress of the nation. They drafted Nigeria's National Pledge, which is often recited after the singing of the national anthem:

> I pledge to Nigeria my country
> To be faithful loyal and honest
> To serve Nigeria with all my strength
> To defend our unity
> And uphold and honour our glory
> So help me God.

We have failed to live up to that pledge.

* * * *

Many Westerners observing the violence in Nigeria attribute it to religious conflict.[2] They argue that the way to eliminate conflict is to do away with religious beliefs. The same people assume that the violence in Rwanda was related to age-old tribal rivalries and say that if we can simply overcome tribalism, all will be well. This chapter has shown that those explanations are far too simple. The violence we live with in Africa has complex roots and is often deliberately fomented by elites who seek to protect their power and wealth. Our awareness of these factors should shape how we set about developing a fully Christian response to it, one that will show sceptics that faith, far from being an impediment to peace, is the road to peace.

Study Questions

1. What stereotypes about other groups exist in your community, and what stories are you told about them?
2. Have any of the politicians in your area used their position to enrich themselves? How have the people around you responded to this?
3. What sorts of things trigger violence in your community? Do they fit under the headings given above, or are there also other sources of violence?
4. What would a Christian response to each of these causes of violence look like?

---

[2] This book is for all who are being persecuted, not only Nigerians. However, many of the readers will be Nigerians, or eager to know more about Nigeria, and accordingly I have included some information about the history of religion in Nigeria in the appendix at the back of this book.

3

PRAYING THE IMPRECATORY PSALMS

African Christians love the book of Psalms. Whatever your mood, you can find a psalm that suits your situation. So on any given day a Christian may pick up the Psalms and find a vivid expression of his or her feelings of the moment, whether discouragement, ecstasy or simply "hanging in there". So it is not surprising that I could find a psalm that gave vent to my feelings after Rev. Tacio Dunio's murder:

> Appoint someone evil to oppose my enemy;
> let an accuser stand at his right hand.
> When he is tried, let him be found guilty,
> and may his prayers condemn him.
> May his days be few;
> may another take his place of leadership.
> May his children be fatherless
> and his wife a widow.
> May his children be wandering beggars;
> may they be driven from their ruined homes.
> May a creditor seize all he has;
> may strangers plunder the fruits of his labour.
> May no one extend kindness to him
> or take pity on his fatherless children.
> May his descendants be cut off,
> their names blotted out from the next generation.

> May the iniquity of his fathers be remembered before the
>   Lord;
> may the sin of his mother never be blotted out.
> May their sins always remain before the Lord,
> that he may blot out their name from the earth. (Ps 109:6–
>   15)

This psalm and others like it are collectively known as the imprecatory psalms. They are psalms in which the psalmists vigorously curse the wicked. Today, there are many preachers who encourage their congregations to read them and pray them against their enemies. We are encouraged to believe that we are entitled to hate "with complete hatred" (Ps 139:22). We are told to call down "Holy Ghost fire" on our enemies.

At one stage, I would have thought this was a legitimate use of these psalms. After all, they are part of God's word, and he put them in the Bible for a reason. Given our suffering, can we not legitimately hate the wicked? Is it wrong to use these psalms to urge young men to fight back?

Today, I would think differently, and for a number of reasons. One of them is that it is all too easy for us to forget that the imprecatory psalms are prayers and so slide into using them as a form of magic. When we pray for "Holy Ghost fire" to consume our enemies, are we not resorting to the old African practice of using witchcraft and incantation to harness spiritual powers to defend us? Is that what God would want us to do?

Using the psalms to curse others also reveals that we do not understand what the book of Psalms is about. These are human words to God, not God's words to us. The writers of the psalms pour out their human emotions to God, including their fear and anxiety in times of danger. Like us, the psalmists speak harshly as they describe their troubles and tell God what they want him to do to their enemies. These are the prayers of troubled hearts appealing for God to intervene in circumstances that are beyond human control. They were never intended to be used like the incantations of traditional religions, which were thought to bring down a curse on one's enemies. We cannot teach that proclaiming these psalms will bring down "Holy Ghost fire" and consume our enemies. Our God cannot be manipulated by incantations.

We also need to remember the theological context in which the psalmists wrote these words. They were very aware of God's promise to Abraham:

> I will make you into a great nation. I will bless you and make you famous, and you will be a blessing to others. I will bless those who bless you and curse those who treat you with contempt. All the families on earth will be blessed through you. (Gen 12:2)

So when the psalmists wrote the imprecatory psalms, they were reminding God of his promise to curse Israel's enemies. But looking at the promise in Genesis reminds us that the goal of God's goal was to establish his kingdom and righteousness on earth. Behind the anger of the imprecatory psalms lies the desire to promote God's justice and righteousness. Look at Psalm 7:6–11:

> Arise, LORD, in your anger;
> rise up against the rage of my enemies.
> Awake, my God; decree justice …
>
> Let the LORD judge the peoples ….
>
> Bring to an end the violence of the wicked
> and make the righteous secure.

The psalmist also prayed that God's judgement would prompt the wicked to seek the Lord (Ps 83:16–18) and provide an opportunity for the righteous to praise God (Pss 7:17; 35:18, 28). It was out of zeal for the Lord and abhorrence of sin that the psalmist called on God to punish the wicked and to vindicate his righteousness. The psalmist was not indulging some personal vendetta.

But we too are suffering, and we too are, supposedly, zealous for the Lord and we too abhor sin. Can we not pray these prayers? Yes, and no.

Yes, we can certainly pray for the coming of God's kingdom. Jesus himself taught us to pray, "Your kingdom come, your will be done, on earth as it is in heaven" (Matt 6:1). But no, we are forbidden to call down curses on another. In Romans 12:14, we are told "Bless those who persecute you; bless and do not curse". We are not to be so filled with anger and bitter jealousy and so captive to the sin of self-interest and the obsession with power and authority that we seek to eliminate our fellow human beings.

If someone urges us to action against our enemies by citing the imprecatory psalms, we must respond by pointing out that the psalmists never ask God to enable them to take vengeance on their enemies themselves. Instead, their prayer is always that God will act on behalf of his people (see Pss 7:6; 35:1; 58:6; 59:5). The power and right to avenge belong to God and to him alone (Deut 32:35).

But, some people will say, the prophet Elijah called down divine fire on his enemies in 2 Kings 1 – why cannot we do the same?

Should we pray every prayer in the Bible? What about Jephthah's prayer in the book of Judges? He too was desperate to win a battle, and so he prayed: "If you give the Ammonites into my hands, whatever comes out of the door of my house to meet me when I return in triumph from the Ammonites will be the LORD's, and I will sacrifice it as a burnt offering" (Judg 11:30–31). Jephthah won a battle, but he had to sacrifice his beloved daughter!

His prayer, like many prayers today, came from anxiety and doubt that the Lord really loved him. Jephthah couldn't believe that he could trust God to do the right thing unless he forced God's hand. Similarly, some of us believe that the Lord will not protect us unless we have a gun in our hand!

The critical challenge for contemporary Christians in Africa is to know the Bible well enough to pray from the Word of God, according to the will of God! That, in essence, is what Jesus meant about giving us whatever we ask for in his name, that is, in accordance with his character of love and righteousness.

Finally, those who are quick to use the imprecatory psalms and call for Holy Ghost fire to fall on their enemies fail to realize that we live in a world where we have myriads of enemies. Eliminating some of them will not solve our problems. For example, many in Nigeria think that the primary problem in Nigeria is Islam. They are quick to mention the Boko Haram sect. So when the founder of Boko Haram was killed by the Nigerian police in 2009, everyone thought that the sect would disappear. That did not happen. In February 2013 when Boko Haram announced a ceasefire, the killings and kidnapping of Nigerians and foreign nationals did not stop. When America succeeded in killing

Saddam Hussein, it was assumed that the Iraqis would embrace peace. When the Taliban in Afghanistan were chased out, it was assumed that Afghans would enjoy freedom. When Idi Amin of Uganda was forced out of Uganda, it was assumed that East Africa would enjoy peace. When the British, French, Portuguese and all colonial masters left Africa in the late 1950s and 1960s, it was assumed that Africa would enjoy unprecedented freedom, development and progress. It is an illusion to hope that getting rid of our enemies will bring peace and prosperity.

Moreover, sometimes we pray the imprecatory psalms without recognizing that we ourselves are our own enemies. On the everyday level, for example, we are often involved in habits that are destructive to our health. We eat and drink "food" that we know is harmful to our system. But it is often easier to pray the way we do because we fail to acknowledge our own wickedness and guilt. If God were to destroy the wicked, we too would be condemned!

We need to pray these psalms, like the rest of the psalms, as an encouragement to the faithful to depend on God at all times and not just during hard times. We also need to encourage each other to leave room for God's grace and mercy.

Study Questions

1. Have you ever prayed one of the imprecatory psalms? What were your motives? What did you hope would happen?
2. Has reading this chapter changed how you think about the imprecatory psalms?

4

THE ROOTS OF VIOLENCE

When I come out of meetings where I hear people talking about the imprecatory psalms, I remind myself that it is good that God's people are turning to Scripture to learn how to respond to issues in their daily lives. What is not good, however, is that many of us are not really interested in finding out what Scripture actually says. Instead, we come to the Bible looking for verses that support our own desires and encourage us to do what we want to do. That is how we end up focusing only on the imprecatory psalms and forgetting Jesus' example and his instruction to pray *for* our enemies, not *against* them.

In the next few chapters, we will try to understand more of what the Bible has to say about violence in both the Old and New Testaments. Such understanding will help us to formulate our response to violence on the basis of all that the Bible teaches, and not merely on the basis of what we want it to teach.

But before we begin, I want to remind you of one important fact. When talking about what the Bible teaches, it is not enough just to quote a series of Scriptures without any thought to the context in which they are found. To explain why, let me remind you of the story of the Ethiopian eunuch (Acts 8:30–35). He was an educated man who could read fluently. But when Philip asked him whether he understood what he was reading, he had to admit that he needed help. We must not be too proud to ask others who have studied the Bible carefully to help us interpret its teachings.

* * * *

Violence occurs early in the Old Testament. We find it in Genesis 4, where Cain murders his biological brother Abel:

> Now Cain said to his brother Abel, "Let's go out to the field."
> While they were in the field, Cain attacked his brother Abel
> and killed him. (Gen 4:8)

Why did Cain do this? He did it because he felt threatened by the fact that his brother was being blessed (Gen 4:4–5).

Jealousy of someone else's prosperity and fear that one is losing out are still powerful incentives to violence. Look back at the sources of violence we discussed in chapter 2. The historical scramble for Africa by colonial powers was set off by jealousy because some European nations were becoming more powerful than others. Today, politicians and warlords scramble to exploit Africa's rich resources of gold and oil and diamonds, and draw others in to fight on their behalf. They tell us that our group is being discriminated against compared to their group, and they feed the flames of prejudice and hostility. Even at the local community level, have we not heard of someone who has prospered being accused of using witchcraft, which is said to justify violence against them and their property?

Violence sparked by jealousy and fear pits brother against brother, neighbour against neighbour, tribe against tribe, until in time the original sources of the conflict are forgotten and all that remains is a long history of violence, nurtured in the stereotypes we cling to and the stories we tell each other.

The story of Cain and Abel and its aftermath illustrates the truth that violence alters relationships of all kinds, including relationships among human beings and the relationship between human beings and God. It affects the identity of both the perpetrators and the victims, and God does not ignore it.

Violence between related groups continues throughout the book of Genesis. We read of conflict among the sons of Noah (Gen 9), between the herdsmen of Abraham and Lot (Gen 13), between Isaac and Ishmael (Gen 21), between Jacob and Esau (Gen 27) and between Joseph and his brothers (Gen 37). These stories involve conflict over things like water resources and the distribution of wealth. They often involve the fear of losing power and control.

As we read the genealogies in Genesis, we see how what began as family feuds led to the division of related people groups into warring nations, many of which end up abandoning the God of their fathers. The Bible clearly knows about the same types of conflicts that trouble Africa.

But the Bible also digs even deeper than the roots of this conflict. It takes us right back to the seed from which all this violence has sprung: Adam and Eve's sin in the garden of Eden:

> What Satan put into the head of our remote ancestors was the idea that they could "be like gods" – could set up on their own as if they had created themselves – be their own masters – invent some sort of happiness for themselves outside God, apart from God. And out of that hopeless attempt has come nearly all that Christians call human history – money, poverty, ambition, war, prostitution, classes, empires, slavery – the long terrible story of man trying to find something other than God which will make him happy.[3]

War has been central to human history because violent instincts are deeply embedded in the human heart.

Satan and his agents encourage the perpetuation of violence and are responsible for the description of history as "a bath of blood".[4] Satan rejoices when men like Lamech celebrate bloody revenge (Gen 3:23–24) and when violence engulfs the world (Gen 6:11). He encourages the vicious circle of violence. To break that circle requires a radical discipleship that is capable of ushering in God's kingdom of peace and love.

Study Questions

1. Compare the roots of violence discussed in this chapter with the roots of violence in Africa that we discussed in chapter 2. What similarities can you see?
2. Read some chapters of Genesis, and see whether any of the situations described there are similar to those you have experienced.

---

[3] C. S. Lewis, *Mere Christianity* (New York: Macmillan, 1960), pp. 53–54.
[4] William James, quoted in Ronald J. Sider, *Non-violence: The Invincible Weapon* (Nashville: W Pub. Group, 1989), p. 93.

5

RESPONSES TO VIOLENCE

By 1987, I was married, had a beautiful baby daughter and was pastoring an ECWA church in Amere, a town about fifty miles away from Kafanchan. Life was hard and we were desperately poor. I tried to grow some crops, but at times food was scarce and we had no money for clothing. Yet we were seeing how God provides for his people in practical ways.

1987 was also the year in which I came face to face with violence. As a boy, I had watched the Igbos flee Kafanchan and seen their homes being looted. I had been frightened by the Biafran War and had cowered each time a plane flew overhead. But now I learnt first-hand what it means to be part of a group that is targeted for annihilation by opposing forces.

There had long been tension between Christians and Muslims in northern Nigeria, with Christians strongly resisting attempts to impose sharia law in the region. Things exploded when a Christian group at a college in Kafanchan invited a Muslim who had converted to Christianity to speak at Easter. During his sermon, he preached and quoted from the Quran. Some Muslims accused him of misinterpreting the Quran. Soon the charge grew to insulting Mohammed. Crowds gathered, the college was set on fire, and Muslims turned on the Christian students, beating them and killing them. The trouble soon spread beyond the college and affected first the whole town and then the whole region. Many lives were lost and many houses, churches and businesses were burnt.

I was safe in Amere, and my parents were relatively safe because their home was some distance from the centre of Kafanchan where most of the looting and rioting took place. Still, I couldn't help but worry as the news reports on the radio came in. At that time, there were no cell phones I could use to contact my parents and the landlines were very poor. I could not even go to them, for the government imposed a five-day curfew, making travel impossible.

The violence did not surprise me. It simply confirmed everything I had been taught about the Hausa-Fulani Muslims, namely that they were evil. And the more I heard about what was happening in Kafanchan, the more my heart burned with hatred and the more I wanted vengeance.

Eventually I managed to find a bus going to Kafanchan. The city was like a ghost town. The bus driver was too afraid even to stop at the bus station and made us get off some distance away. I hurried to my parents' house. They were safe, but they had seen the smoke rising from burning buildings and had heard the cries of the victims and the perpetrators. Some of their neighbours had headed to the city centre to try to defend their fellow Christians against attack. My parents had also lost their only source of income, for the market had been burnt. There was nowhere for my mother to sell the wood she gathered or the produce from their small farm.

Worst of all was the news that the Rev. Tacio Dunio, the vice-president of my denomination, ECWA, had been struck down with a machete. This was a man who had dedicated himself to the gospel of peace. He loved the Lord with all his heart and served him faithfully. Was it right that he should die like an animal at the hands of evil people? My heart was filled with anger and pain.

At his funeral, the president of the denomination told us to be strong and turn the other cheek. I thought he was talking nonsense! The only thing I wanted was vengeance. The church leaders kept saying, "God will take care of it". Which was clearly nonsense, because God obviously hadn't taken care of it. If he had, Rev Dunio would still be alive, and so would many other Christians.

I had spent two years working as a herd boy for Fulani Muslims, and I knew how they thought of us. So I was not surprised to learn that in the violence they had targeted minority tribes such as mine. They thought we were inferior and our Christian faith made us infidels. I had no doubt that the Muslims hated us and wanted to enslave us with their religion. If we did not submit and adopt Islam, we would be annihilated, either physically or economically. In Muslim majority areas, Christians struggled to get into universities and even to find any sort of job.

As I walked around the devastated city centre and spoke to people, my mind raged and my heart was filled with anger at every injustice (real and perceived) that I'd ever suffered at the hands of Muslim Hausa-Fulani.

Still, I had much to be grateful for. As the reports were coming in, it seemed to me that the Christians in Kafanchan had retaliated against the Hausa-Fulani community. I was really happy about that. Christians in other towns in the state had not fared so well. In places like Funtua and Kaduna, Igbos had been especially attacked for they were a predominantly Christian tribe. Many of them had fled, just as they had done when the Biafran War started.

I have told this story at length to show that the way I as a young pastor reacted to violence was not very different from the way young men are reacting to violence against Christians today. This is the natural way to respond – with hatred, a belief that what we have seen confirms all our stereotypes about others, and a delight in vengeance. It is a very human response.

But is it a Christian response? Jesus explicitly told his disciples that they were to be different from other people:

> You have heard that it was said, "Love your neighbour and hate your enemy." But I tell you, love your enemies and pray for those who persecute you, that you may be children of your Father in heaven. He causes his sun to rise on the evil and the good, and sends rain on the righteous and the unrighteous. If you love those who love you, what reward will you get? Are not even the tax collectors doing that? And if you greet only your own people, what are you doing more than others? Do not even pagans do that? Be perfect, therefore, as your heavenly Father is perfect. (Matt 5:43–48)

When we resort to cursing our enemies, are we not behaving exactly like everyone else? How are we then different from those Muslims who pray only for their fellow Muslims? I have heard blind beggars in Zamfara State saying, "Allah ya kiyaye Musulmi" ("May Allah protect Muslims"). Their words imply that only Muslims deserve God's mercy and compassion. Does Scripture encourage us to pray like this?

Study Questions

1. How have you responded when violence has affected you? Be honest as you describe your response.
2. In what ways are your responses to violence the same as those of your enemies?

6

OPPRESSED AND OPPRESSORS

Earlier, I said that the authors of the imprecatory psalms were looking back to God's covenant with Abraham in Genesis 12:1–2. But that was not their only point of reference. They were also looking back to the book of Exodus and its account of how God intervened on behalf of Israel in Egypt and punished the Egyptians and their rulers. These events gave them confidence that God acts on behalf of those who cry out to him for help in times of trouble.

God Acts When His People Are Oppressed

In the first half of the book of Exodus, we see God's people being oppressed by their enemies, and then miraculously delivered when God steps in to act for them. This is the type of action we want to see! It is the type of action that leads some to declare that God is on the side of the oppressed – and when we feel that we are being oppressed, we like to think that God is on our side. We can use this claim as a rallying cry to draw others in to fight alongside us.

But one thing we need to note as we read Exodus is that the Israelites did not do very much to deliver themselves from oppression. Moses, their leader, did not arrive with a rebel militia to deliver them. He arrived in Egypt accompanied only by his brother and armed with his shepherd's staff. And he came reluctantly, because God had told him to go, not because it was his life's ambition to deliver his people and rise to a position of leadership (Exod 3–4). He did not organize a rebellion and try to spread terror among the Egyptians. Yet because God was with him, he was able to confront Pharaoh and eventually lead the people out as God had commanded him to (Exod 5–13).

Even after leaving Egypt, Israel faced great danger. Pharaoh and his army were fully armed and eager to take Israel back to captivity or destroy them. The people were terrified, but they obeyed Moses when he told them

> Do not be afraid. Stand firm and you will see the deliverance the LORD will bring you today. The Egyptians you see today you will never see again. The LORD will fight for you; you need only to be still. (Exod 14:13–14)

Then Moses went into action. He stretched his hand out over the water as God told him to do and the Red Sea parted so that the Israelites could pass through it in safety.

Does anything about this sequence of events remind you of Jesus' teaching? Maybe not immediately, but you may see the parallels if you think about Jesus' teaching about not retaliating when we are attacked. Moses did not lash out at the Egyptians himself. He committed himself and his people to God's care.

But we should also note that not retaliating is not the same thing as being completely inactive or passive when under attack. Moses had to stretch out his hand over the sea and the Israelites had to walk through the sea to the other side. Jesus is not asking us to be passive when we face violence. We can take action, but not violent action. That should be left in God's hands. God, and not the Israelites, was the one who destroyed the Egyptian army.

In the days and years that followed, the Israelites moved through wild country as they journeyed to the promised land. Some of those they met along the way attacked them and the Israelites were allowed to defend themselves (see, for example, Exod 17:8–16). But it is important to remember that by this time Israel was a nation, and as such it was entitled to defend itself against other nations who attacked it. The forces Joshua led while Moses prayed for them were the equivalent of a disciplined army, not an unruly mob or a group of rebels.

Sometimes, we focus on self-defence. During one of the crises in Jos in the Plateau State, a friend of mine attended a meeting of denominational leaders who were discussing how to respond to the crisis. After deliberating on how to meet the victims' immediate need of food, water, shelter and clothing, the leaders moved on to discuss how to protect their congregations. They were encouraged to have a load of stones delivered to their church premises so that they could use them to repel attackers. Someone suggested that they should collect head pans like those women use to carry loads and use them as shields against stones being thrown during attacks.

Those who argue in favour of self-defence point to the example of Nehemiah, whose men kept their swords girded on to ward off attacks as they rebuilt the wall of Jerusalem (Neh 4:18). They argue that this justifies our holding the Bible in one hand and a gun in the other.

But if you read the book of Nehemiah, you will realize that he did not depend on those swords or on military strategies to defend the nation. He and his people continued to focus on the God of Israel, who was capable of defending them and the city they were rebuilding.

Moreover, we are not living in the same time period as Nehemiah. We know about Jesus, whom Nehemiah did not know. And Jesus has taught us that we need to be both as wise as snakes and as harmless as doves. We need to master the art of creative, non-violent self-defence.

God Acts When His People Become Oppressors

We rejoice that God delivers the oppressed. But what happens when the oppressed become oppressors? In the books of Judges and Kings and in the writings of the prophets, we see that happening. The people stopped paying close attention to what God had said through Moses and instead did whatever they wanted. They became proud and exploited their neighbours and other nations, and they paid the price.

In some ways, the situation of the Israelites who settled in the promised land was similar to the situation in Africa after we first gained our independence. A new nation was being formed, and people were struggling with the transition from one way of life to another. For the Israelites, the shift was from being nomadic pastoralists to settling down to life in villages and towns. For us, the shift has been from a united struggle against colonial powers to working together to take responsibility for our own destiny.

Times of transition are always challenging. It is very easy to decide that the old rules and the old moral codes no longer apply. That is what the Israelites did as they forgot about the law of Moses with its commands about justice and righteousness. They preferred immorality, idolatry and bloodshed. Many in Africa have followed the same course.

But God had warned the Israelites against forgetting him and drifting into sin. He had told them and taught them by experience that he punishes sin, regardless of who commits it. The elite cannot flout him, and nor can his chosen people. He had warned them of the consequences of disobedience, and God keeps his promises. He does not lie. That is why there is a recurring pattern in the book of Judges: The people sin; God sends enemies to subdue and oppress them; the people repent; God delivers them from their enemies. The same pattern continued throughout the history of ancient Israel and in the history of the church. It seems that Satan is constantly trying to lure God's people away from him. His attacks do not only take the form of persecution by outsiders; he also tries to spread corruption and immorality within the church. He rejoices when he can persuade us to abandon Christ's plain teaching on non-violence and take up arms. He is even happier when he can persuade us that we are justified in oppressing others. He is the one who is cheering when Christian youth take revenge by killing innocent Muslim passers-by.

The prophet Ezekiel gives one of the clearest answers to the question with which we opened this chapter: If God is on the side of the oppressed, what happens when the oppressed become oppressors?

> The sin of the people of Israel and Judah is exceedingly great; the land is full of bloodshed and the city is full of injustice. They say, "The LORD has forsaken the land; the LORD does not see." So I will not look on them with pity or spare them, but I will bring down on their own heads what they have done. (Ezek 9:9–10)

God created all things to bring him glory; violence desecrates what God made good. So God hates violence and bloodshed. Those who perpetrate it are guilty of the sins of murder and abomination. That thought did not cross my mind when I cheered on those who were taking revenge on ordinary Muslims in Kafanchan. I was not seeing violence from God's perspective, and being holy as he is holy. I was not working to bring his kingdom here on earth.

Judges and Kings

Those who are eager to fight may argue that the books of Judges and Kings contain accounts of leaders who fought battles on behalf of God's people. That is true. But as my comments on the nation have made clear, we should not take those times as the model for our behaviour today. In the times of the judges, the nation was deeply sinful.

Moreover, we should not forget that not every judge was a military leader. Some like Gideon were certainly warriors. But there are others, like Tola and his successor Jair about whom nothing more is said than that they judged Israel for twenty-three years and twenty-two years (Judg 10:1–4). It seems that these men delivered and judged Israel not by winning military victories but by placing themselves at the head of the tribes and preventing the recurrence of hostile oppression through the influence they exerted, as well as by what they did for the establishment of the nation in its fidelity to the Lord.

What then about David? There can be no doubt that he was a great king and a great warrior who also served and loved God. His warlike life can cause confusion for Christians who oppose violence.

First, we need to remind people that David was the leader of a nation. Before he became king, he was a general in the army. And he did not come to power in a coup d'état – in fact, he deliberately avoided taking that route (see, for example, 1 Sam 24:1–7). He exercised his power within an official structure.

Moreover, if we look at David's hymn of praise in 2 Samuel 22, we get a better idea of the man. He was someone who could distinguish between primary causes and secondary causes. His skill in combat, his fortresses, his physical strength and agility all of these were gifts from God. But none of them guaranteed him success. He knew at the deepest possible level that he owed all his victories in battle to God's help. Yet even a man like David could fail to use his power wisely. He used violence to cover up his own sins (2 Sam 11:14–15) and he let his success make him want to brag about the size of his army, which is why he conducted a census (2 Sam 24:2). Both actions led to nothing but trouble for David and for his people.

David's pride did not let him admit that he had sinned with Bathsheba. His pride made him count his army. In the same way, our pride can lead us to refuse to listen to what Jesus says. It is pride that makes us say that we know better than God, and that we have no more cheeks to turn.

We may insist that we need to say this so that our enemies know that we are ready to fight. But while we are sending that message to our enemies, we are sending a very different message to God. We may say that we are acknowledging him, but we are like those who pay a *kobo* worth of false humility to get a *naira*[5] worth of pride toward others.

Study Questions

1. In what way do you think saying that we have no cheeks to turn could constitute pride?
2. How have contemporary Christians understood the life of warriors like Samson and David, or prophets like Elijah?

---

[5] Nigerian currency.

7

JESUS AND THE KINGDOM OF GOD

In an earlier chapter, I mentioned the Ethiopian eunuch who needed help understanding what he was reading (Acts 8:27–35). The particular passage he was looking at when Philip met him was Isaiah 53:7–8:

> He was led like a sheep to the slaughter,
>> and as a lamb before its shearer is silent,
>> so he did not open his mouth.
> In his humiliation he was deprived of justice
>> Who can speak of his descendants?
>> For his life was taken from the earth.

The "he" referred to in this passage is the Suffering Servant who faced suffering and pain with dignity. The way some pastors use the imprecatory psalms to urge young men to confront the enemy shows that they do not grasp the true nature of the Servant in Isaiah. As Christians, we are called to follow the Prince and Saviour of the church who resolved to absorb suffering and pain to save us and to model a non-violent response to violence.

Jesus himself took his "job description" from Isaiah. We see this in the famous scene in the synagogue in Nazareth:

> He went to Nazareth, where he had been brought up, and
> on the Sabbath day he went into the synagogue, as was his

custom. He stood up to read, and the scroll of the prophet Isaiah was handed to him. Unrolling it, he found the place where it is written:

"The Spirit of the Lord is on me,
because he has anointed me
to proclaim good news to the poor.
He has sent me to proclaim freedom for the prisoners
and recovery of sight for the blind,
to set the oppressed free,
to proclaim the year of the Lord's favour."

Then he rolled up the scroll, gave it back to the attendant and sat down. The eyes of everyone in the synagogue were fastened on him. He began by saying to them, "Today this scripture is fulfilled in your hearing." (Luke 4:16–21)

As far as this book is concerned, what is really interesting here is what Jesus does *not* say. You see, he was reading from Isaiah 61:1–2, but he does not read all the words in those verses. If you look at the passage in Isaiah, you will see that verse does not only speak of proclaiming "the year of the Lord's favour" but also of proclaiming "the day of vengeance of our God". Those are the words that those who love to quote the imprecatory psalms want to hear. But Jesus refused to say them. Why? John's Gospel gives us the answer. Jesus insists that he "did not come to judge the world but to save the world" (John 12:47).

The "poor" to whom Jesus proclaims "good news" are both the oppressed and the oppressors, both the victims and the victimizers. While the oppressed are victims of violence, the perpetrators of violence are also captives of violence. Both groups desperately need deliverance. So the good news Jesus brings concerns the oppressed and the oppressors. Christians who use the imprecatory prayers today tend to assume that God is only compassionate and merciful to the victims and not to the perpetrators. But all of us need salvation.

In his mercy and compassion God can bring even the perpetrators of violence to a life-changing encounter with Jesus Christ, and sometimes even use them to bring blessing to many. Saul of Tarsus, who later became the Apostle Paul, is a prime example. He was in the forefront of persecuting the early Christians (Acts 8:1–3; 9:1–2; Phil 3:6). But when he met Christ he became an instrument of God and ended up writing much of the New Testament.

God is still doing the same thing today. There is, for example, the testimony of the former terrorist who uses the pseudonym "Ray". Ray was part of a Middle Eastern terrorist group, committed to creating an Islamic state. He was even eager to be a suicide bomber. When he and his group found some Christians who were converting others, they seized all their books and evangelistic materials. But instead of destroying the books, Ray started to read them, with growing interest. Then one night he had a dream. He was in a place

> where all the prophets were sitting on horses near me. I started asking questions about who they were, and they said they were Abraham, Jacob and Isaiah. Then I asked who the other was and they said, 'This is Jesus'. And then I said, 'Wow, this is Jesus, this is Jesus?' I was so excited and so happy. When He removed the veil from his face, I was so … I was full of the Holy Spirit in my life. I felt so strong and started to shout, 'Jesus! Jesus! Jesus!' It was amazing, the joy and the strength I had inside my heart. I was laughing and laughing and then I woke up from the dream, and my pillow was full of tears.[6]

The salvation of people like Ray and the Apostle Paul demonstrates that God's compassion and mercy extend not only to the victims of violence but also to the perpetrators of violence. God's compassion and mercy knows no bounds. He loves with an extreme love, a radical love even in the wake of violence. Jesus did the same.

But, you may say, that is all very well for God the Father and Jesus the Son. But I am human, and I have to live on earth. I am not God and I cannot act like God. Unfortunately, Jesus does not buy this argument. He instructs us to imitate him and pray for, bless and love our enemies:

> You have heard that it was said, 'You shall love your neighbour and hate your enemy.' But I say to you, Love your enemies and pray for those who persecute you, so that you may be

---

[6] http://www.opendoorsca.org/content/view/290/139/

children of your Father in heaven; for he makes his sun rise on
the evil and on the good, and sends rain on the righteous and
on the unrighteous. For if you love those who love you, what
rewards do you have? And if you greet only your brothers and
sisters, what more are you doing than others? Do not even the
Gentiles do the same? Be perfect, therefore, as your heavenly
Father is perfect. (Matt 5:43–48)

What Jesus is saying is that in our world it is ordinary to love our friends
and family while shunning or hurting our enemies. But the world Jesus
envisions – the kingdom of God – is different. Everyone is invited into
the kingdom, even people we may despise. God gives good things (like
sun and rain) to everyone, regardless of whether they are just or unjust.
So we should be like God and respond with love even to those who
promote injustice.

Jesus' command is the first reason we need to refrain from responding
to violence with violence. But there are also other reasons why we
should learn to love rather than hate. The first is that all human beings,
including even our enemies, are God's creation and are made in his
image (Gen 1:27). That image was damaged at the fall, but traces of it
remain. If God still loves his fallen creatures, can we do less? Do we not
have a responsibility to protect God's creation?

Secondly, we need to remember that the all-powerful God does not
need our violence. The Apostle Paul reminds us of this when he says,
"Do not take revenge, my dear friends, but leave room for God's wrath,
for it is written: 'It is mine to avenge; I will repay,' says the Lord" (Rom
12:19; quoting Lev 19:18; Prov 20:22). We can trust him to bring
evildoers to justice in his own time, even if, like the saints in Revelation,
we cry out, "How long, Sovereign Lord, holy and true, until you judge
the inhabitants of the earth and avenge our blood?" (Rev 6:10). The
book of Revelation makes it clear that his judgement will come.

Finally, there is something that we remind ourselves of each time
we follow in Jesus' footsteps and pray the Lord's Prayer, the prayer
that Jesus taught his disciples to pray, and ask God to forgive us as
we forgive others (Matt 6:12). Each time we say these words, we are
reminded that we are sinners like those who sin against us. Almost all
of us have the potential to turn on our neighbours and so stand in need

of God's mercy. How can we pray for God's wrath on others when we ourselves were once children of disobedience (Rom 11:32)? If God had not shown us mercy, we would have been dead by now. If that is the case, why should we deny others the privilege of receiving God's mercy?

Like Jesus, we must pray: "Father, forgive them, for they do not know what they are doing!" (Luke 23:34). He did this even while enduring one of the cruellest methods of execution. His follower Stephen was one who learnt this lesson. As he was being stoned, he prayed, "Lord, do not hold this sin against them" (Acts 7:60). In doing this, he shows us that he had come to have the mind of Christ.

By this stage, those of you who are in the same state of mind as I was in after the violence at Kafanchan will be angry. Does God just want to stand there and let our enemies kill us? Are we merely to let our hands hang down and do nothing to protect our people?

No. That is not what I am saying. We will look at our options in more detail later in this book. But for the present, let me remind you that the Gospels show that while Jesus did not resort to violence, he was committed to promoting both God's love and God's justice. His commitment to the truth of God's love for all people led him to consistently and boldly challenge injustice whenever he encountered it. Challenging injustice is not inconsistent with loving those who are responsible for that injustice. "Love" is not always the same as "being nice". For example, taking away someone's car keys would be a better way of showing love than avoiding a confrontation by letting them drive drunk. Taking their keys away may save their life and the lives of others.

Study Questions

1. Has there been a time when you have struggled to pray the Lord's Prayer because of what it says about forgiveness?
2. Give an example of a time when you tried to respond to physical or emotional violence with love.
3. Read one of the Gospels, focusing on how Jesus responded to his enemies and to oppressors. Share your observations with others.

8

FROM HATE TO FORGIVENESS

I told you about the hatred that welled up in my heart in 1987. I did not act on it, but nor did I deal with it. But the violence persisted, and could not be ignored. In 1992, religious violence flared again. This time, the spark that lit the tinder of longstanding grudges between the Hausa Muslims and Christian Katafs was the relocation of a market in the small town of Zangon-Kataf. In the ensuing violence, the town was destroyed.

As news of the riots spread through the entire Zaria region, Christian congregations far from Zangon-Kataf suddenly found themselves being attacked during Sunday services. Tachio Duniyo, the pastor of the ECWA church on Amina Road, and many of his congregation were killed, and the church and its manse were burnt to the ground. The police offered no protection; they simply stood by and watched the rioters. Similar scenes took place at other churches.

Hundreds died, including my neighbour, Bobai Tokan. He was a committed Christian, a member of my denomination. We attended some church activities together. Many of us in the church admired his family life. One of my pastor friends was eager to marry his daughter.

As a Christian leader, who would soon become the Church Council Secretary of ECWA, I said the right things, but my heart was not in it. I was aware that my words about forgiveness and not retaliating carried little power because I was only half-convinced of them myself. I focused my energy on helping churches cope with the forces that wanted to crush northern Nigerian Christians under their heel.

At the same time, I was applying for a grant to study in the USA. When that came through, I found that it would cover only 70% of what was needed, and so I had to devote my energy to finding the remaining funds. My life was full, what with my work and my growing family, for we now had two daughters. But I still had time for my cousins, and particularly for Ishaya Bobai Aniya. We were close, for we were both in Christian ministry. When I was at last able to leave to take up my scholarship, he rejoiced with me – and I promised him that once there I would try to find a way for him to join me so that we could study together and return together to bless Nigeria with what we had learnt.

In 1999 I bade a tearful goodbye to my family and boarded a plane that would take me to Philadelphia. Little did I know that I would be gone for seven years, with only brief visits home, before I completed both an MDiv and a PhD.

I did not forget my promise to Ishaya and eventually our plans fell into place. I would return home briefly in 2001 when I finished my MDiv, and then he would travel back to the USA with me. He had admission to the college and the finances were falling into place. We would share accommodation to reduce our costs.

But tension was building again in Nigeria. Twelve states in the northern region decided to impose sharia law on all those who lived there. In some of these states, like Kaduna, roughly half the population was Christian. They would face considerable hardship if sharia law was introduced. For example, Christian women would not be able to catch any bus that arrived but would be forced to wait until eventually a women-only bus arrived. And that was only one of the many difficulties they would face under sharia law.

In January 2000, Christians staged a peaceful protest against the imposition of sharia law and went to deliver a letter to the state government in Kaduna. But the protesters were violently attacked by Muslim youths. In the days of carnage that followed, thousands died, including at least twenty Christian priests and pastors. Among them was my cousin Ishaya. A mob broke into his home, seized him and slashed his throat while his two young children watched in horror before fleeing to a neighbour's house. His church was set on fire.

I was meeting with one of my professors when my phone rang and I heard the message I dreaded: "Ishaya is dead! We do not know what has become of your brothers."

My professor knew me well, and he knew Africa well. When I told him what had happened, he too was devastated. We bowed our heads and wept and prayed together. In his grief and anger, he prayed, "Rise up, O God. Avenge the blood of your servants! Send down fire on these who have attacked them. Just burn them, destroy them." It was a prayer I had heard before in Nigeria, and one I had uttered myself.

But this time, I could not say Amen to his prayer. I was no longer the person I had been in 1987. Then, I knew very little about theology and the Bible. But in the course of my studies, I had learnt much about what Jesus did, how Jesus thought, what Jesus would expect us to think, and how Jesus would expect us to treat our enemies. Almost to my own surprise, I found myself praying, "God forgive the Muslims for what they have done and spare them. They don't know what they are doing, and they have no hope."

I meant those words. God had indeed transformed my heart.

My professor knew far more about Jesus and the New Testament than I did. But, as I had done earlier, he was following his emotions rather than Christ when he prayed. When he heard my prayer, he was humbled. I gently said to him, "We can't continue this way, we can't continue with hatred because it will not take us anywhere. We just need to trust God, we need to ask God. God knows how to handle these people."

Writing about this incident in *Christianity Today* magazine, Craig Keener says,

> I bowed my head in shame. Sunday's compassion was right. And for the safety of millions of our brothers and sisters like Sunday, as well as for those Muslims, we need to keep praying for peace – and speaking for truth.[7]

Study Questions

1. Give thanks to God for the measure of insight he has already given you into how to respond to violence, and pray for more.
2. Pray for your enemies, and for peace.

---

[7] Craig Keener, "Mutual Mayhem". *Christianity Today*, November 2004.

9

SPEAKING FOR TRUTH

The change in my attitude to violence came about because of my education. Does that mean that education will end violence? No. In the years before Nigeria became independent in 1960, the regional government in northern Nigeria launched a mass literacy program that was known as the War against Ignorance (*Yaki Da Jahilici*). It was believed that the spread of education would dispel cruelty and build mutual trust and love as people gained knowledge and insight. Today, there are educational institutions in every community across the country. But there has been no corresponding decrease in cruelty in the twenty-first century. Instead, we have seen the rise of the group known as Boko Haram (a name that means "Western education Is Forbidden") which has killed countless Christians and Muslims and abducted their children. Education alone is not enough to end violence.

The change in my attitude to violence is also rooted in my religion. Does that mean that spreading religion will end violence? No. Africans are already very religious. Religion on its own will not make us respect human life and love our neighbours.

Was it the fact that I am a Christian that made a difference? Yes – but Christianity alone is not enough. I was already a Christian when I supported those who killed Muslims. The rapid spread of Christianity in Africa has not reduced the violence on this continent. It is not only Muslims who have committed atrocities in Nigeria. And we should not forget that Christians were active participants in the massacres in Rwanda.

As Dr Keener recognized, it is not enough just to be educated or to pray – we also need to keep "speaking for truth", and specifically for the truth of the Bible – the whole Bible. As we noted at the start of this book, the traditional religions of Africa instilled fear as the most compelling reason for ethical action. If one did not obey the teachings of one's people, one would endure the wrath of the gods and of ancestral spirits. Christianity liberated us from that fear and taught us to fear God. It also taught us that God is love, and that forgiveness is easy. What it often did not teach is what it means to be a disciple and to have our minds transformed by God's word. So while we were undoubtedly believers, we still tended to think in ungodly ways, which led to ungodly action. This makes it extremely difficult for Christians to imitate and model Christ's humility, love, patience, endurance and forgiveness. This problem is not unique to African Christians.

Some may object to what I have just said. After all, evangelical Christians in Nigeria and elsewhere in the continent are generally known as conservative Christians who hold firm to the doctrine of biblical inerrancy and the coherence of biblical truth. Their passionate faithfulness to biblical truth is demonstrated in their rejection of the Western postmodern spirit of relativism, with its lack of absolutes. Conservative evangelicals are strong voices in the gay and lesbian debate in Africa and have spoken out boldly against the celebration of gay and lesbian marriage in Europe and North America.

Unfortunately, some of these same conservative evangelicals are rejecting other parts of the Bible, and particularly Jesus' teaching on turning the other cheek. For example, after the bomb blasts in Jos in 2011, I had a conversation with some retired pastors. During their time in active pulpit ministry, they had encouraged members to face persecution with prayer and courage. So I was taken aback to hear them assert that turning the other cheek was no longer an option. They said to me, "Sunday, make sure when Muslims burn two churches, you burn four mosques." Such words coming from retired pastors carry a lot of weight with younger men!

And these retired pastors are not alone in their view. It is a view shared by some Christian leaders. A renowned Pentecostal pastor, John Praise, has called on churches to encourage young people to defend the church because no one has a monopoly of violence. "People say, when they slap your cheek, you turn the other. We have turned both, and they have slapped us. There is nothing else to turn."[8] The voices of those encouraging retaliation are often stronger than the voices of those arguing that Christians must resist such temptation and that fighting back is contrary to the position of our Lord Jesus Christ. As a result, some church leaders have been training youth to counter attacks from Muslims. A northern Christian militia named Akhwat Akwop emerged in September 2011 vowing to match "blood for more blood, violence for more violence, and life for more lives".[9]

Those who encourage a violent response to violence are blind to the evil practices that often accompany counter-attacks and reprisal attacks. The young men who go to battle lose sight of God, and resort to the standard practices of traditional warfare as they prepare for battle and as they fight. They forget that Jesus and Paul non-violently challenged social and political injustices throughout their ministries, and encouraged peace-making rather than retaliation. Jesus says, "Blessed are the peacemakers, for they will be called children of God" (Matt 5:9). He told Peter to forgive those who sin against you "not seven times, but seventy-seven times" (Matt 18:22). Many Christians today no longer pay attention to these Scriptures.

To illustrate how violence has changed the way Christians think about biblical teaching, we can use the analogy of leprosy. Leprosy destroys its victims' nerves. When the nerve cells are damaged or destroyed, there is no feeling. Thus when the fingers or toes are injured, there is no pain. When the eyes are rubbed too hard or otherwise injured, there is no pain. With no pain, there is no care for the cut or injury and infection sets in. The infection eventually rots the flesh or destroys the eyes. So the ravages that lepers suffer are not from the disease, but from the lack of care of injuries and subsequent infection, because the sufferer feels no pain. Conflict violence has had the same effect across Africa. It destroys Christian moral nerves and the resulting sin destroys the church.

We need to listen carefully and patiently to the suffering that leads some to turn from the Bible. Only then can we speak for the truth and

---

[8] John Praise as quoted by Sunday Oguntola in "Church Leaders Debate Self-Defense: Nigerian Christians Abandon Cheek-Turning", *Christianity Today*. December 2011, Vol. 55, No. 12, p. 14. Available online at http://www.christianitytoday.com/ct/2011/december/self-defense-debate.html.

[9] Emeka Ibemere, "Nigeria: Christian Group Vows to Fight Boko Haram". *All Africa*, 29 September 2011. Available online at http://allafrica.com/stories/201109290623.html.

clearly teach what the Bible says about violence – not just in one place, but as its overarching theme. Part of our response to violence must be the cultivation of biblical literacy in ourselves and in those to whom we minister.

Study Questions

1. What do you think the author means by "biblical literacy"?
2. Are you biblically literate? If not, what can you do to address this problem?
3. Think about the metaphor of violence as leprosy. Does it accurately reflect the situation?

10

THE BIBLE AND SUFFERING

One important area in which we need to speak for truth concerns the truth of suffering. Many are confused about this. Their confusion is evident in the words spoken by someone I once heard leading a time of devotion. He said that he had never seen a child of God suffer. Then he asked, "Has anyone seen a true child of God suffer?" Nobody said anything. I waited to see whether anyone would speak up and call his attention to what Scripture teaches, but there was silence. They all accepted what he was saying as true or were too afraid to speak up, knowing that if they mentioned any case of suffering, the speaker would promptly use the suffering as proof that the sufferer was not a true child of God. This is a circular argument that no one can win!

This speaker is not the only one to think like this. Many in the current generation of African Christians have adopted a mind-set that is totally opposed to all human crises and suffering. This was evident at the funeral of a Christian brother who died of liver disease. During the eulogies, one of his colleagues announced that the Bible says whatever a Christian decrees shall stand. So he decreed that his colleague's death would be the last death in the family and in the community. Almost half of the congregation said, "Amen!" – a word that means "Agreed, yes indeed or let it be so, on the basis of the Word of God." Yet this man's decree is contrary to the Word of God! God has decreed that every human being will face death.

When I listen to Christians making assertions like those I have just described, I am left with the feeling that we listen to Scripture with headphones on – and the music we are hearing from our iPods and mobile phones is so loud that we can't hear what Scripture is actually saying. This negative attitude to suffering, which is widespread today, is one of the reasons we find it so difficult to accept Jesus' teaching about loving our enemies.

Our response to anyone who says that no true child of God will suffer is that Jesus was surely the ultimate true child of God. And he undoubtedly suffered. It was his love, suffering, death and resurrection that make it possible for us to have our sins forgiven and be reconciled with God and our neighbours.

But, some will say, Jesus suffered so that we don't have to. That is true to the extent that Jesus suffered so that we do not have to endure the ultimate suffering of eternal separation from God. But his death does not mean that we escape suffering in this world. Think of another true child of God, the Apostle Paul. Do you remember what he suffered? Here is his own description of his life, which includes much suffering that is not even mentioned in the book of Acts:

> I have worked much harder, been in prison more frequently, been flogged more severely, and been exposed to death again and again. Five times I received from the Jews the forty lashes minus one. Three times I was beaten with rods, once I was pelted with stones, three times I was shipwrecked, I spent a night and a day in the open sea, I have been constantly on the move. I have been in danger from rivers, in danger from bandits, in danger from my fellow Jews, in danger from Gentiles; in danger in the city, in danger in the country, in danger at sea; and in danger from false believers. I have laboured and toiled and have often gone without sleep; I have known hunger and thirst and have often gone without food; I have been cold and naked. (2 Cor 11:23–27)

That does not sound like an enjoyable way of life! But Paul could also write, "I consider that our present sufferings are not worth comparing with the glory that will be revealed in us" (Rom 8:18).

But, some will again object, such suffering was a consequence of Paul's being an apostle, but we ordinary Christians should not expect to suffer like that ourselves. Paul would disagree. When he was preaching to "ordinary" believers in the towns of Lystra, Iconium and Antioch, he told them that "We must go through many hardships to enter the kingdom of God" (Acts 14:22).

To understand why this is the case, we need to remember that although we enjoy God's eternal salvation, we still live in a world that is full of sin and suffering. Paul speaks of it as subject to frustration and decay, and says that it is not only we humans but also the entire creation which groan for liberation (Rom 8:20–25). We have not yet entered God's perfect world where God "will wipe every tear from their eyes" and "there will be no more death or mourning or crying or pain" (Rev 21:4). That wonderful world is still in the future. In the meantime, we have to live humbly, hopefully and patiently as we participate in his plans for the final redemption of the whole of creation.

We also need to read the text of the Bible carefully. We love the verse that says "He who did not spare his own Son, but gave him up for us all – how will he not also, along with him, graciously give us *all things*?" (Rom 8:32). We like to think of "all things" as including a car, a house, a family, security, food and so forth. But "all things" can also include suffering! In Philippians 1:29 Paul clearly states, "For it has been granted to you on behalf of Christ not only to believe on him, but also to suffer for him." No wonder when Paul speaks about his goal of knowing Christ, he also speaks about sharing his suffering (Phil 3:10–11).

So we should not be surprised when we experience suffering and pain. They are part and parcel of the salvation package. It follows that we cannot use our suffering as an excuse to ignore Christ's radical teaching on forgiving our enemies and those who cause us pain.

Unfortunately, many Christians prefer prosperity teaching and "luxury Christianity". Gone are the days of the Acts of the Apostles when believers thanked God for the privilege of suffering for his sake (Acts 5:41) and prayed for perseverance and determination in the face of suffering (Acts 4:23–31). We need to relearn what it means to model Christ's humility, perseverance, love and forgiveness in the face of undeserved suffering.

We learn this not just by speaking about it theoretically but by looking at examples of people who have lived this way – and not just people in the distant past, but people in the present. For example, we need to hear more stories like that of Elias Chacour.

Elias was born into a Palestinian Christian family in 1939. When he was eight, he and his family were displaced by the Israelis to the village of Gish. He was awakened one night by the sound of angry voices blaring over loudspeakers: "Come out of your houses. We want all men to come out and give themselves up. You are leaving here at once." Elias' father and brothers were arrested and taken away.

In the months that followed, Elias' heart ached for his missing father and brothers. But one hot day as he sat alone under an olive tree thinking about them, he remembered words his mother had said to him, "Blessed are those who mourn, for they will be comforted." Then he imagined Jesus walking towards him, saying those words. For the first time, the words began to make sense. Elias began to pray to Jesus: "Mother has your comfort. I can see that. But can't you just speak a word and make all this trouble go away? Do you want us to be your lips and hands and feet – as Mother prays – to bring peace again? If that's true, you can use my hands and feet. Even my tongue." He also prayed for his father and brothers to come home. Three months later, they were reunited. But there was much more suffering to come.

One day, Israeli soldiers roared into Gish again, looking for a thief they believed had cut and stolen some telephone wire from the new kibbutz they were building. They grabbed Elias and other children and began to beat them, accusing them of the crime. But as the Israeli soldiers beat and cursed him as a filthy, worthless Palestinian, Elias heard another voice too, saying, "Blessed are you when people falsely say all kinds of evil against you ... for in the same way they persecuted the prophets who were before you." A few days later the wire was found. It had been cut accidentally, and the Palestinian boys had nothing to do with its disappearance.

Elias Chacour became an ordained priest and served Christ for years in a little church in Galilee. He has received an international peace award and has travelled the world, preaching the gospel and speaking on peace and justice, leading non-violent demonstrations and working for reconciliation between Palestinians and Israelis, whom he refers to as his "brothers and sisters."[10]

---

[10] Adapted from *Prayer Devotional Bible*, NIV (Grand Rapids: Zondervan, 2004), p. 1304.

Elias Chacour lives in the Middle East. Where are his African counterparts? We need to tell the stories of ordinary men and women, boys and girls, who have faced the reality of persecution and suffering and can still see their oppressors as "brothers and sisters" because of their own deep trust in and love of God.

Here is one such story:

In September 2001, the Rev. Sunday Gomna's house and church in Jos were set on fire. He lost all his belongings. His congregation rebuilt the church, and a year later it was again destroyed by fire. They rebuilt again, and endured vandalism, the theft and destruction of church property, and the church being used as a toilet and a rubbish dump by the Muslim community. Through all this, Rev. Gomna stood firm in his opposition to violence. And because he himself has suffered great loss, he could set a powerful example of non-retaliation and forgiveness. Instead of burning a mosque, his congregation started a medical clinic that served their Muslim neighbours. Rev. Gomna worked tirelessly to build relationships with Muslims in the community. Eventually, his Muslim neighbours were the ones protecting the church, ensuring that no one would steal, vandalize or throw rubbish on its property.[11]

Study Questions

1. Do you know any "Elias Chacours" or "Sunday Gomna's"? If so, tell their story to others.
2. If you do not know anyone like them, reflect on what the absence of such stories implies about how closely you and your community are following the example of Jesus.

---

[11] More details about this story and others like it are told in a book by Yakubu Pam and Katrina Korb. *Fighting for Peace: Learning from the Peace Heroes among Us* (Jos: Fab Educational Books/ YACPIF, 2011).

11

THE WAY OF JESUS

Words and action have power. Non-violent action is not passive.
— Leah Wells

Jesus clearly told his disciples to expect suffering:

> If the world hates you, keep in mind that it hated me first
> … Remember what I told you: "A servant is not greater than
> his master." If they persecuted me, they will persecute you
> also. … In fact, the time is coming when anyone who kills you
> will think they are offering a service to God. … I have told you
> this, so that when their time comes you will remember that I
> warned you about them. (John 15:18, 20; 16:2, 4)

What did Jesus tell them to do in response to such suffering? They were
to continue to testify to him in the power of the Spirit (John 15:27) and
they were to live in a way that demonstrated that in him they had peace.
After all, he told them,

> I have told you these things, so that in me you may have peace.
> In this world you will have trouble. But take heart! I have
> overcome the world. (John 16:33)

We listen to these words, and we agree with them. But what does all of
this mean in practical terms when it comes to day-to-day life? Jesus did
not spell this out for his disciples when he was speaking to them on the
night before he died. He did not need to. The eleven men to whom he
was talking had lived and travelled with him for almost three years by
this time. They had already watched him respond to everyday violence

(although even they were not ready for his response to the terrible violence that would engulf him shortly after he said these words).

But we have not had the same experience as the disciples. Where can we find out how to respond to the violence around us? The answer is that we can read the Gospels and see how Jesus handled various types of situations. We can also listen to the teaching Jesus gave to the crowds who followed him. In particular, we can listen to his words in the Sermon on the Mount

> You have heard that it was said, "Eye for eye, and tooth for tooth." But I tell you, do not resist an evil person. If anyone slaps you on the right cheek, turn to them the other cheek also. And if anyone wants to sue you and take your shirt, hand over your coat as well. If anyone forces you to go one mile, go with them two miles. Give to the one who asks you, and do not turn away from the one who wants to borrow from you. (Matt 5:38–42)

When we read these words, we need to remember the context in which Jesus spoke them. His people, the Jews, were being ruled by the Romans. Their situation was as bad or worse than that of Africans enduring colonial rule or Christians living in Muslim areas. An ordinary Roman soldier could just grab hold of a Jewish man and force him to carry the soldiers' pack for a mile while the soldier strolled along at ease behind him, or kicked and cursed him if he stumbled. The Jewish man was treated like a pack animal. When we are suffering at the hands of others, do we not often complain that we are being treated like animals?

The people who followed Jesus were not only mistreated by the Romans but also by their own religious and political elites, who despised them, and let them know it. In John's Gospel, we hear the leaders referring to the people who followed Jesus as "this mob that knows nothing of the law" and saying that there was "a curse on them" (John 7:48).

Jesus' hearers were like many of us in that they did not have a voice in the halls of power. They were treated as second-class citizens, just as Christians are in Muslim areas. They were led to feel that they were worthless in the sight of other people and God.

These are the people whom Jesus tells to turn the other cheek! Why? Surely he should have been telling them to rise up, slap the person who slapped them, curse those who cursed them, and assert that they had rights just like their oppressors had rights? But instead he says,

> You have heard that it was said, "Love your neighbour and hate your enemy." But I tell you, love your enemies and pray for those who persecute you, that you may be children of your Father in heaven. He causes his sun to rise on the evil and the good, and sends rain on the righteous and the unrighteous. If you love those who love you, what reward will you get? Are not even the tax collectors doing that? And if you greet only your own people, what are you doing more than others? Do not even pagans do that? Be perfect, therefore, as your heavenly Father is perfect. (Matt 5:43–48)

He is telling them that they must not respond to oppression by adopting the behaviour of the oppressors. They do not need to be equal to their oppressors; they need to be better than them!

Think about it. Most of the Jewish people in Jesus' time were denied access to state and economic power. They were systematically and psychologically frustrated and persecuted. They were oppressed in their motherland, both by the Roman authorities and by their own religious and political leaders – the Pharisees, Sadducees, Herodians and others. They knew first-hand what it meant to suffer oppression and domination. They hated their oppressors to the core. They grew up believing that powerlessness was their lot in life. Therefore, they were helpless, incapable of changing their situation; all was incurable.

This is the way many Christians feel in northern Nigeria. In fact, a recent report identified a sense of extreme helplessness and dependence on the goodwill of others as one of the problems facing the church in northern Nigeria.[12]

So was Jesus adding to people's sorrows, troubles and hopelessness by asking them to turn the other cheek? Not, at all! In teaching about turning the other cheek, Jesus was essentially stating the obvious to help

---

[12] Arne Mulders, "Summary of the research report 'Crushed but Not Defeated: The Impact of Persistent Violence on the Church in Northern Nigeria'" prepared for Open Doors International, February 2014.

them understand a not-so-obvious principle of life in a violent context. He wanted them to know that they could non-violently force their oppressors to recognize their human dignity. He illustrates this with three examples.

Example 1: Turning the Other Cheek

The first example involves turning the other cheek. Jesus' point is that when someone gives you a contemptuous slap, you neither cower in fear nor react with uncontrolled anger. Instead of just reacting, you act with dignity. We see Jesus himself do this when he is on trial for his life before the high priest:

> When Jesus said this, one of the officials nearby slapped him in the face. "Is this the way you answer the high priest?" he demanded.
>
> "If I said something wrong," Jesus replied, "testify as to what is wrong. But if I spoke the truth, why did you strike me?" (John 18:22–23)

Does that give you a better idea what it means to "turn the other cheek"? It certainly does not mean that we simply accept any injustice done to us. It does mean that we respond with dignity, and are free to appeal to the law and to justice. That may not be enough to deliver us – Jesus was still condemned at this trial. But he did not allow others to dehumanize him. Instead he challenged them to recognize the injustice of their actions.

You may be surprised to know that we even see an example of this in the Old Testament. It happened when a prophet named Micaiah was warning the king against going to war, a course of action that certain false prophets, led by Zedekiah, were encouraging him to take:

> Then Zedekiah son of Kenaanah went up and slapped Micaiah in the face. "Which way did the spirit from the LORD go when he went from me to speak to you?" he asked.
>
> Micaiah replied, "You will find out on the day you go to hide in an inner room."

The king of Israel then ordered, "Take Micaiah and send him back to Amon the ruler of the city and to Joash the king's son, and say, 'This is what the king says: Put this fellow in prison and give him nothing but bread and water until I return safely.'"

Micaiah declared, "If you ever return safely, the LORD has not spoken through me." Then he added, "Mark my words, all you people!" (2 Chr 18:23–27)

Micaiah did not strike back at Zedekiah, or curse him and call down divine fire on the false prophets. He simply stated a truth. Even when the king ordered him imprisoned, Micaiah had the last word, and he spoke it not only to the king but to all who were present.

It may also be significant that Jesus speaks of someone slapping you "on the *right* cheek".[13] In general, such a blow would have been administered with the back of the left hand. In Jesus' day, as today in parts of Africa, it was not polite to touch food or a person with one's left hand. A blow administered with the left hand was contemptuous and was meant to humiliate and wound the spirit rather than the body. But when the one struck presents the left cheek to be struck too, the attacker has to switch to his right hand. This is the hand that would be extended to an equal. Will he use that hand against one he despises? Simply by forcing the attacker to make that decision, the one struck reaffirms his or her human dignity.

Those who turn the other cheek are thus neither passive nor cowardly. Would you call Sunday's Gomna's Christians "cowardly" when they rebuilt their burnt church, and painted the words "Father, forgive them, for they do not know what they are doing" on the wall behind the altar? Would you call them "passive" when they established a medical clinic for their Muslim neighbours?

---

[13] For a more detailed examination of this point, see Walter Wink, *Engaging the Powers: Discernment and Resistance in a World of Domination* (Minneapolis, Minnesota: Fortress Press, 1992), p. 176–177.

Example 2: Going the Extra Mile

If turning the other cheek is an assertion of human dignity in the face of oppression, going the other mile is an assertion not only of dignity but of caring about one's oppressor as a person, or in other words, showing love for them. In effect, the one being forced to carry the soldier's pack for them is saying, "I acknowledge that you have treated me like an animal. I am tempted to throw your pack down now that I have carried it for one mile, and to go off cursing you as a Gentile dog. But you are a man like I am, and I am prepared to voluntarily offer you help if you need it (and in the process I will rescue someone else from being forced to carry your pack)."

How do you think a soldier would react to someone who spoke like that? He can demand his pack back, saying that he is quite competent to carry it himself, in which case he is being forced to acknowledge the humanity of the person he had regarded as beneath contempt. Or he may get an inkling of what God's kingdom is like when he meets someone whose actions are characterized by compassion, love, justice, peace, forgiveness and reconciliation, rather than by hatred, anger and a thirst for revenge.

The prophet Isaiah was talking about the kingdom of God when he wrote, "How beautiful on the mountains are the feet of those who bring good news, who proclaim peace, who bring good tidings, who proclaim salvation, who say to Zion, 'Your God reigns!'" (Isa 52:7). Peace is associated with the reign of God. Peace is also associated with good news, salvation and good tidings. No wonder, Jesus Christ lived and preached the gospel of peace in a world of oppressive structures, which prompted hatred and violence against fellow human beings. He invites Christians to preach the gospel of peace today, and one way he suggests they do this is going the extra mile.

Let me give you an example of what this could mean in practice, again drawing on what happened at Rev. Sunday Gomna's church. During worship one Sunday, a Muslim boy threw a stone and smashed the windscreen of a church member's car. The boy was apprehended by neighbours and marched off to the local police station. When Sunday Gomna arrived at the police station, he recognized the boy and took him home. He then negotiated with the boy's father and the owner of the vehicle. They agreed to split the costs of the repair between them, for the boy's father was a poor man and could not afford to pay the full amount. Even paying for 50% of the cost would impose a severe burden. So imagine the man's reaction when Rev. Gomna raised the amount that was owing and gave it to him to pay off his debt! Both father and son were amazed. As news of what had happened spread, the incident became a turning point in the relationship between Christian and Muslim communities in the area.[14]

Example 3: Giving Your Cloak

In what circumstances would someone have wanted to take away someone's cloak in Jesus' day? The answer is probably that this would happen if someone was in debt. There are some people so poor that all that they own are the clothes on their back. Deuteronomy speaks of such people when it talks of someone offering his cloak as a pledge for a debt (Deut 24:12–13) and commands that the cloak should be returned at night so that the poor person can at least sleep under it, using it as a blanket.

Presumably, the scene Jesus envisages is one where someone is ignoring the law of Moses and has gone to court to claim possession of a coat that was given in pledge for a loan. In the face of such contempt for God's law, the debtor has no option but to hand over this cloak, but he then strips off his undergarments as well, hands them to the astonished man who is suing him and walks out of the court naked!

Can you imagine the scandal. Everyone would hear what had happened. And everyone would know that the rich man had been willing to strip a poor man of everything that he owned. He would have been condemned for his actions. He would have been the one to be shamed, rather than the poor man who was left naked.

The effectiveness of this tactic is clear from the fact that it is exactly what some otherwise powerless women in Africa have sometimes done to draw attention to their cause. It was used in the Women' War against the British colonial forces in Eastern Nigeria in 1929 and it was used

---

[14] Pam and Korb, *Fighting for Peace*, pp. 73–74.

in Delta State by women protesting against companies that were not fulfilling their social responsibilities.

Summary

Walter Wink suggests that Jesus' instructions can be summed up as follows:[15]

- Seize the moral initiative.
- Find a creative alternative to violence.
- Assert your own humanity and dignity as a person.
- Meet force with ridicule or humour.
- Break the cycle of humiliation.
- Refuse to submit or to accept the inferior position.
- Expose the injustice of the system.
- Take control of the power dynamic.
- Shame the oppressor into repentance.
- Stand your ground.
- Force the Powers into decisions for which they are not prepared.
- Recognize your own power.
- Be willing to suffer rather than retaliate.
- Force the oppressor to see you in a new light.
- Deprive the oppressor of a situation where force is effective.
- Be willing to undergo the penalty of breaking unjust laws.

The examples Jesus used show that he was not telling his disciples to accept whatever abuse is handed out to them and run away rather than confront oppressors. Instead, he was providing an alternative approach to violence that embodies one of the central purposes of God's kingdom: non-violent direct engagement with the structures of injustice in society. The fact that he does so through examples, as we have stressed above, means that we have to work out how to do this in each new context. These are not meant to be "one-size fits all" responses. Like Jesus, we have to be creative and use our minds to work out the best way to reject injustice while also expressing our love for those who persecute us.

---

[15] Walter Wink, "Jesus & Alinsky", January 05. http://www.nthposition.com/jesusampalinsky.php.

Sometimes, this may even involve organizing a football match! That was what was done in Jos in 2010. A week-long football camp attracted both Christian and Muslim students, who competed in interfaith teams and took part in peace activities and discussions. The winning team was awarded the Peace Cup – but the entire community won as many young men were transformed from people who followed the crowd into violence to people who actively work for peace, and no longer demonize people of a different faith.[16]

Study Questions

1. Use your imagination to enter into each of the examples Jesus gives. Act out these scenes with a friend.
2. After doing this, ask your friend how he or she felt, and consider other possible responses.
3. Watch for scenes of confrontation or humiliation in your home or place of work or community. Then spend some time meditating on what responses the one being humiliated could have made to affirm their dignity and to show love for their oppressor.

---

[16] Pam and Korb, *Fighting for Peace: Learning from the Peace Heroes among Us*, pp. 13–17.

12

SO WHAT DO WE TEACH?

As shown in the previous chapter, turning the other cheek is not a call to passivity but to creativity. There is a lot of creativity in Africa. Unfortunately, some of it is misapplied. For example, on a recent trip to Abuja, I was told that some Christians are making a creative argument based on Ephesians 2:8–9. There Paul says, "For it is by grace you have been saved, through faith – and this is not from yourselves, it is the gift of God – not by works, so that no one can boast". Because salvation is by grace, these creative Christians argue, God will not refuse Christians entrance into heaven because they sin. Therefore, they are free to disobey Jesus' teaching on turning the other cheek. After all, they say, to adhere to this teaching is to try to be saved by works and that, as we all know, is impossible for no one is perfect. So it does not matter if they take up arms rather than folding their hands and allowing Muslims to destroy the church and its members.

Their statement that we are saved by grace is correct. But that does not leave them free to sin. Those who misuse Ephesians 2:8 are forgetting that the very next verse says, "We are God's handiwork, created in Christ Jesus to do good works, which God prepared in advance for us to do" (Eph 2:10). And these "good works" include obeying Christ's call to love and serve our neighbours and pray for our enemies.

The mere fact that this verse is ignored is a reminder of the lack of depth in much Christian preaching and teaching today. Preaching is often directed merely to people's emotions and does nothing to help them understand the meaning of salvation or what it means for their everyday life. Even if there is application to life, it can be very limited and legalistic in its scope. As pastors see the moral laxity in the church and society, their frustration leads them to preach simple, legalistic messages that do not allow for deeper reflection on ethics and non-violence.

Prosperity preaching is also rampant. I was at a church service where 98% of the pastor's message was on how to name your offering and claim your blessings. The preacher was saying that if we expect a blessing from God, we must give an offering that matches what we expect. The message was aimed at the people's perceived and felt needs and targeted their emotions. There was nothing in it that taught them sound doctrine so that they could grow in the grace of God.

So one of the first things we need to do is to take the time we spend in worship on Sundays seriously. No one who reads and deeply reflects on Psalm 73 can take worship lightly. After expressing his frustration with the way God treats the wicked, the psalmist concludes:

> Surely in vain I have kept my heart pure
> and have washed my hands in innocence.
> All day long I have been afflicted,
> and every morning brings new punishments. (Ps 73:13–14)

But his perspective was transformed when he entered the sanctuary of God:

> If I had spoken out like that,
> I would have betrayed your children.
> When I tried to understand all this,
> it troubled me deeply
> till I entered the sanctuary of God;
> then I understood their final destiny.
>
> Surely you place them on slippery ground;
> you cast them down to ruin. (Ps 73:15–18)

The pastors in our churches need to remember that worship should be a time when lost visions are recovered, human potential is redefined, and believers are strengthened, encouraged and sharpened. Pastors who lack this perspective may use the worship time to serve their members "junk food". But worship should be a time when we "quicken the conscience to the holiness of God; … fill the mind with the truth of God; … open the mind to the love of God; ... purge the imagination by the beauty of God [and] devote the will to the purposes of God".[17]

If you are a pastor or leader, these five points could serve as a checklist for any worship you lead. Are you supplying those who come to your church with the antibodies they need to resist being infected by the violence around them? Unless we do so, they will continue to question the realism of some of Jesus' teachings. Those whose minds have not been filled with the truth of God and the love of God and whose imaginations have not been purged by the beauty of God will not devote their wills to the purposes of God.

To put this another way, we must give our congregations some idea of what it means when we pray "Your kingdom come" as part of the Lord's Prayer. For too many, these words could be paraphrased as "I would like to live in paradise". But they are not only a prayer for God to intervene and make everything right; they are also a prayer that we may work to bring in God's kingdom of holiness, justice, peace and love. So we need to teach in a way that gives church members a clearer grasp of God's kingdom perspective and of moral values and that encourage them to take part in non-violent direct engagement with the structures of injustice in society.

As part of this teaching, we will need to remind them that God is a God of peace. It is Satan who promotes war and violence. That is why Paul ended his letter to the Christians in Rome with the words, "The God of peace will soon crush Satan under your feet" (Rom 16:20). Paul's words remind us of God's promise in Genesis 3:1 that Eve's descendant, Jesus, would crush Satan's head to allow humanity and the rest of creation to enjoy God's peace.

As the God of peace, God wants church people to love one another and their neighbours, including those who hate them. That is what Jesus taught and modelled in his own life.

But, you may ask, why is love so important? For an answer to that question, we can look at Paul's great hymn to love in 1 Corinthians 13:

> Love is patient, love is kind. It does not envy, it does not boast, it is not proud. It does not dishonour others, it is not self-

---

[17] William Temple, former Archbishop of Canterbury.

seeking, it is not easily angered, it keeps no record of wrongs. Love does not delight in evil but rejoices with the truth. It always protects, always trusts, always hopes, always perseveres. Love never fails. (1 Cor 13:4–8)

The words "Love never fails" sum up what he has been saying. Only love has the capacity to guarantee that peace and joy will continue. Thus love, peace and joy are among the core moral values of Christ's kingdom.

Paul clearly saw the danger and the destruction that awaits the Christian community if it fails to grasp the importance of these things in God's kingdom perspective. And so he urged the Roman Christians

> And now I make one more appeal, my dear brothers and sisters. Watch out for people who cause divisions and upset people's faith by teaching things contrary to what you have been taught. Stay away from them. Such people are not serving Christ our Lord; they are serving their own personal interests. By smooth talk and glowing words they deceive innocent people. (Rom 16:17–19, NLT)

To young men, war may seem glamourous and appealing, but it is nothing of the kind. The fact that it appears so is part of Satan's deception. He loves to gloss over the role that the leaders' personal interests play as they incite us to take up arms.

Jesus told the Jews of his day, who lived with the experience of powerlessness, to turn the other cheek. He was not asking them to passively accept inhumane and unjust treatment. Rather, he was encouraging them to engage non-violently with their oppressor until he or she recognized their human dignity. Thus, Jesus was introducing a radical change. He opened their eyes to a new reality, a rising sun of hope for the poor. This principle was capable of transforming the incurable circumstances of life. Jesus' instruction was a radical call to discipleship that offers hope in the midst of conflict and destruction. We should issue the same call to those to whom we preach.

Study Questions

1. Think about the services in which you have participated (as a leader or as a member of the congregation) over the last month. Which of the functions of worship identified by William Temple have they fulfilled? Which have they not fulfilled?
2. Think about the idea of God's kingdom. What does it mean for us to pray that the kingdom of God will come in the here and now, rather than in the distant future?

13

SO WHAT DO WE DO?

Jesus knew what was coming. He knew that his disciples would suffer and that the early church would have to endure war and persecution. He knew that someday Christians in Nigeria would be confronted by an Islamic sect that would see them as evil and bomb their churches and institutions. So while persecution may not be normal, we should not be surprised when it comes. African Christians are not the first nor are they going to be the last to be hated and persecuted for their faith in Jesus Christ. So one way for us to feed our own creativity when it comes to responding to violence is to learn more about how believers in the past have responded to it.

The writer of Hebrews devoted a whole chapter to the cloud of witnesses who have endured persecution for the sake of their faith in God and their willingness to serve his purposes (Heb 11). He knew, as we need to remember, that persecution does not destroy the church; it is sin that does that. That is why the Apostle Peter urged the early Christians to remember what Jesus had taught:

> Do not repay evil with evil or insult with insult. On the contrary, repay evil with blessing, because to this you were called so that you may inherit a blessing. For,

> "Whoever would love life
>   and see good days
> must keep their tongue from evil
>   and their lips from deceitful speech.

> They must turn from evil and do good;
>> they must seek peace and pursue it.
> For the eyes of the Lord are on the righteous
>> and his ears are attentive to their prayer;
> but the face of the Lord is against those who do evil."
>> (1 Pet 3:9–12; quoting Ps 34:12–16)

Peter did not promise the Christians wealth and prosperity; instead, he said they would suffer for doing what is right and just. Yet "even if you should suffer for what is right, you are blessed" (1 Pet 3:14a). When he wrote those words, Peter may have been remembering words he himself had heard Jesus say, and had struggled to understand:

> Blessed are you when people hate you, when they exclude you and insult you and reject your name as evil, because of the Son of Man. Rejoice in that day and leap for joy because great is your reward in heaven. (Luke 6:22–23)

Peter was not writing to "super-Christians" but to people like us. He recognized that they, like us, were experiencing fear and tension and all the emotions that disorient Christians and can cause them to respond to violence with counter-violence. So Peter urged them, "Do not fear their threats; do not be frightened" (1 Pet 3:14b). These too were words that Peter had often heard Jesus say to him and the other disciples (see, for example, Matt 10:26–31; 14:30; 17:7).

So Peter was not exhorting people to do something he had not done himself. In the book of Acts, we read about Peter and other apostles being persecuted by the Jewish leadership and commanded to stop preaching. But "the apostles left the Sanhedrin, rejoicing because they had been counted worthy of suffering disgrace for the Name [of Christ]" (Acts 5:41). They actually rejoice that they were given the privilege to share the fellowship of Christ's suffering and pains! The Apostle Paul was the same. One of his key goals was to know Jesus Christ and have the great privilege of participating in the fellowship of the suffering of Christ (Phil 3:10).

Christian tradition tells us that both Peter and Paul died for their faith during the days of the Emperor Nero. The reasons they were persecuted sound very familiar to us today. They were scapegoats, identified as the ones to be blamed for what was going wrong in the Roman Empire. Similarly, some Muslims today blame Islam's decline on Western secularism, which they link with the rise of Christianity. So they persecute Christians. In northern Nigeria, the spread of Christianity was also seen as a threat to the political, economic and religious establishment there, which is why that is the region where persecution is concentrated.

Emperor Nero took the same tack and played the blame game:

> In 64 AD, a great fire ravaged Rome. Nero took the opportunity provided by the destruction to rebuild the city in the Greek style and begin building a large palace for himself. People began speculating that Nero had set the fire himself in order to indulge his aesthetic tastes in the reconstruction.[18]

To shift the blame, Nero accused the Christians of having started the fire and launched the first government-sanctioned persecution of believers. According to the Roman historian Tacitus,

> Besides being put to death they [the Christians] were made to serve as objects of amusement; they were clad in the hides of beast and torn to death by dogs; others were crucified, others set on fire to serve to illuminate the night when daylight failed. Nero had thrown open his grounds for the display, and was putting on a show in the circus, where he mingled with the people in the dress of a charioteer or drove about in his chariot.[19]

But Nero's plan to blame the Christians backfired. Tacitus continues his account of their suffering with these words:

> All this gave rise to a feeling of pity, even toward men whose guilt merited the most exemplary punishment; for it was felt that they were being destroyed not for the public good but to satisfy the cruelty of an individual.

Nero made it a capital crime to be a Christian. But his barbaric treatment of Christians did not wipe out the faith. Christianity continued to thrive

---

[18] http://www.religionfacts.com/christianity/history/persecution
[19] Henry Bettenson and Chris Maunder, eds., *Documents of the Christian Church*, 3rd. ed. (Oxford UP, 1999), p. 2.

and blossomed. God used the situation to raise the level of love for Christians and Christianity. Christianity became a popular religion. The church gained power and made many converts. From then on, Christians were resolute in defying any policy that ran counter to the Word of God.

In the centuries that followed "many Christians chose to die before they would deny their Lord. Those who did so came to be called martyrs or witnesses."[20] Their ability to absorb suffering and pain and to face persecution with courage and boldness contributed to the conversion of the scholar Tertullian to Christ in the second century AD. He would go on to become one of that century's chief theologians. His most famous work was addressed to Roman magistrates and was a powerful defence of Christianity and of Christians. In it, he profoundly observed, "The blood of the martyrs is the seed of the church."

Tertullian came from Carthage in North Africa. About ten years after his death, another great man emerged in that city. He was St. Cyprian who was elected bishop at a time when the church in Carthage was enjoying peace and prosperity. But the very next year severe persecution broke out, and continued intermittently for a number of years. Christian leaders were targeted. At first, Cyprian went into hiding so that he could continue to lead the flock, but he could not do this indefinitely. So he courageously took the lead, writing books to encourage the believers and defending the faith in person. He reminded his flock that "this temporal and brief suffering … shall be exchanged for the reward of a bright and eternal honour".[21] When he was condemned to death by the sword in AD 258, he responded by saying, "Thanks be to God!"

What was the reason for this official persecution of Christians? In later years, it was not that they were being blamed for evil deeds (as Nero had suggested) or that the Roman Empire was intolerant of other religions:

> The Roman Empire was generally quite tolerant in its treatment of other religions. The imperial policy was generally one of incorporation – the local gods of a newly conquered area were simply added to the Roman pantheon and often given Roman

---

[20] www.religionfacts.com/christianity/history/persecution
[21] From *Epistle* 76, *Ante-Nicene Fathers* 5.

names. Even the Jews, with their one god, were generally tolerated. So why the persecution of Christians?[22]

The answer to that question is linked to the way the Romans understood the role of religion. "For the Romans, religion was first and foremost a social activity that promotes unity and loyalty to the state – a religious attitude the Romans called *pietas,* or piety."[23] That is why the Roman authorities felt so strongly about the need for Christians to conform to the laws of the state and offer a sacrifice to the emperor if this was demanded of them. To refuse to do so was to disrupt the social order. Cicero felt so strongly about this that he wrote that "if piety in the Roman sense were to disappear, social unity and justice would perish along with it."

The Jews also refused to sacrifice to the emperor, but they were tolerated because their faith was an ancient one. However, Christianity, which started out as a branch of Judaism, was increasingly recognized as a new religion, and thus when Christians refused to make sacrifices their religion was branded as a dangerous superstition, that would spread sedition and disloyalty. As such, it was to be eradicated.

A similar motive for persecution exists today. Africans also link ethnicity, culture and religion – as I did when I assumed that all Fulani were Muslim and thus hostile to Christians. We also see this in the insistence that northern Nigeria is Muslim and southern Nigeria is Christian. We may protest that in six northern Nigerian states Christians constitute at least 50% of the population. But such statistics are not even discussed; they are simply dismissed as irrelevant by those who insist that the north is Muslim by definition. When those of the "wrong" group are present in a region, they are mistrusted, persecuted, and blamed for any actions taken by coreligionists.

Social values still determine who is "in" and who is "out" of the circle of ethical and moral obligations. Those who are labelled inferior can be targeted for genocide or ethnic cleansing with impunity. Thus Christians are persecuted in Nigeria and elsewhere because Muslims view Christianity as an inferior, Western religion. Christians, in turn,

---

[22] www.religionfacts.com/christianity/history/persecution
[23] www.religionfacts.com/christianity/history/persecution, citing Robert L. Wilkin, "The Piety of the Persecutors," *Christianity History*, Issue 27, Vol. XI, No. 3, p. 18.

stereotype Muslims. This mutual stereotyping has resulted in mistrust and ongoing suspicion.

Although most of the persecution endured by the early church was carried out by legitimate governments, which is not the situation in Sub-Saharan African today, Christians in Nigeria and elsewhere in Africa can still learn from their early cousins who showed tremendous resilience in the face of terrifying persecution. Their faith in the possibility of change kept them going. They firmly believed that the suffering and pain in this world are temporary.

Moreover, their response to persecution had positive side-effects. It "facilitated the rapid growth and spread of Christianity, prompted defences and explanations of Christianity ... and ... raised fundamental questions about the nature of the church."[24] Sadly, as the church continued to grow numerically, its attitude to violence changed. Centuries later, the Christians engaged in counter-attacks and even launched crusades against the Muslims. The bitter fruit of those crusades is still flourishing today, poisoning relations between Christians and Muslims. The non-violence of the early church accomplished more for the kingdom of God than the violence of their successors.

We can learn from the early church's reliance on prayer and fasting in response to persecution. Prayer, fasting and worship were their method of self-defence. In situations where they had to choose between denying their Lord Jesus Christ or dying for him, people like Peter, Paul and Polycarp (the bishop of Smyrna – died AD 155) were prepared to pay the price for living for Jesus in a decaying and broken world.

But that was not all that the early Christians did. There were those among them who took up their pens and carefully defended the faith by writing and engaging in debates and dialogues. They explained to the pagan world who Jesus was and what the Christian practices and beliefs meant. They refuted rumours that the Christian "love feast" involved sexual orgies, and that the sacred meal in which they ate bread and wine in honour of Christ's death involved cannibalism. They realized that their oppressors were ruled by ignorance, and that ignorance kills.

---

[24] Kenneth Scott Latourette, *A History of Christianity,* Vol. 1 (Peabody: Mass; Prince Press, 2000), p. 81.

Similarly, we need to understand the issues of our day and objectively face those issues in our theological and political reflection. Christians and Muslims need to engage in careful public debate and dialogue on the issues that are destroying the African continent. Not all of us will have the skills to write books, or the training to analyse the issues, or the public profile to be invited to appear on television or speak on the radio. But those who do these things are continuing the role of the early Christian "apologists". We can support them in prayer, and learn from what they say so that we are not at a loss when we are challenged about our beliefs.

The great witnesses who have gone before us left us a legacy that we must continue to reflect upon. No one who carefully reads the stories of the persecuted saints of the early church can fail to reflect deeply on his or her attitude to the sin of violence and to the grace of God. Such stories encourage us. As we delve into the history of the church and of Nigeria, we will find that those who persecute Christians do not succeed in wiping out the church.

Study Questions

1. What aspect of the suffering of the early Christians most closely matches your experience?
2. Try to find out some information about one Christian martyr who lived in a previous century anywhere in the world, including Africa. Tell others about the aspect of their response to suffering that speaks to you or amazes you.

14

DOES NON-VIOLENCE WORK?

The early church absorbed the impact of all forms of persecution by adopting a pacifist stance. But that is not the only way in which non-violence can manifest itself. Each generation of Christians has to think of creative strategies for dealing with violence in a way that remains faithful to Christ's will. Such obedience is a true mark of radical discipleship.

Unfortunately, Christians have not always been the ones who have taken the lead in this. It has sometimes taken non-Christian political leaders to make us recognize that the type of response to violence that Jesus advocates is capable of overthrowing dictatorial systems. Let us look at three men, two of whom were not Christians, who were in a weak position and used non-violence to fight for their people's rights.

Mahatma Gandhi

Mahatma Gandhi (1869–1944) was not a Christian. His interest in the faith was extinguished by the behaviour of those who claimed to be Christian (a solemn warning to us). But Gandhi admired Christ and was drawn to his teaching. Thus he was influenced by Christ's words in the Sermon on the Mount when he said that "violence cannot be destroyed by counter-violence. Mankind has to get out of violence only through non-violence. Hatred can only be overcome by love."[25] Accordingly, he led his people in campaigns against oppressive colonial

---

[25] Harijan, July 7, 1946.

practices and oppressive local traditions. He not only worked for India's independence but also sought to alleviate poverty, expand women's rights, and end the caste system. What he achieved was a non-violent revolution that overthrew a century of British colonial rule in India. By the time Gandhi was assassinated, the British king could no longer claim to be the Emperor of India.

Martin Luther King Jr.

The story of Martin Luther King Jr. (1929–1968) is a testament to the workability of the ethics and morality of non-violence when faced with oppressors from within one's own country. The oppression he was facing was race-based. The United States of America had never fully turned away from its slave-owning past, and there was great discrimination against black people in that country, even though they had been there almost as long as their white oppressors. Black people faced threats to their human dignity and personhood. They were sometimes treated like animals, denied education and killed without any attempt to bring their murderers to justice. Thousands of people were enduring this oppression despite a constitution that declared that all people were equal. Does that sound at all similar to the oppression some of us are enduring in Nigeria?

God raises people to represent him in times of persecution. In the USA, he raised up Martin Luther King Jr., a Baptist pastor born in 1929. His conviction that all men are brothers enabled him to recognize the humanity of both the oppressed and the oppressors. He believed that both were victims of the schemes of the devil and both were thus in need of deliverance.

Dr King came on the scene at a time when some were overwhelmed by the injustice and passively accepted it while others were advocating violent opposition. Dr King was able to overcome the temptation to return hate with hate. He believed that the principle of non-violence is capable of turning things around. His visit to Mahatma Gandhi further confirmed and fortified his belief: love, not hate, changes sour and warped social relationship. He believed in what Jesus said to his disciples, "If you have faith as small as a mustard seed … nothing will be impossible for you" (Matt 17:20–21).

He was imprisoned for his social activism. But from the jail in Birmingham, Alabama, King eloquently spelled out his theory of non-violence: "Non-violent direct action seeks to create such a crisis and foster such a tension that a community, which has constantly refused to negotiate, is forced to confront the issue."

Martin Luther King Jr. received the Nobel Peace Prize in 1964. Although he was assassinated in 1968, Martin Luther King Jr. is now celebrated across the globe. His speech, "I Have a Dream" continues to impact both America and other societies.

Nelson Mandela

Nelson Mandela (1918–2013) tried both non-violent resistance and violent resistance and learnt from experience that only non-violence works to relieve the suffering and pain caused by our fellow human beings. His story is amazing. It helps African Christians understand that although the roots of social discrimination, labelling and stereotyping are deep, they can be uprooted. It shows that dehumanizing social values can be fought with dignity and faith in Christ's principle of non-violence.

Nelson Mandela was born in South Africa in 1918. He grew up in an environment where the human dignity of Africans was not recognized. So Mandela studied law to prepare himself for life in such a society. He joined the African National Congress (ANC) in 1942 with the goal of working with others to transform the organization into a non-violent grassroots movement that would eventually bring apartheid to its knees. He became a spokesman for the millions of rural peasants and workers who had no voice under the apartheid regime. The poor gave him their full support.

Recognizing that the ANC's earlier tactics of polite petitioning were ineffective, he and his colleagues suggested a review of the method. In 1949, the ANC officially adopted the Youth League's method of boycotts, strikes, civil disobedience and non-cooperation. Their goal was to achieve full citizenship for Africans, redistribution of land, trade union rights, and free and compulsory education for all children.[26] Mandela devoted twenty years of his life to directing "a campaign of peaceful, non-violent defiance against the South African government and its racist policies, including the 1952 Defiance Campaign and the 1955 Congress of the People". He and his colleagues were often charged with treason and imprisoned.

By 1961, Mandela was frustrated at the lack of progress being made and lost patience with his earlier approach. He felt that the non-violent protests were not achieving anything and began to assume that an armed struggle was necessary to get the attention of the apartheid regime. He proceeded to become the co-founder of Umkhonto we Sizwe (MK), an armed offshoot of the ANC dedicated to using sabotage and guerrilla war tactics to end apartheid. He orchestrated a three-day national workers strike in 1961, for which he was arrested and sentenced to five years in prison. He was again brought to trial in 1963, and at what became known as the Rivonia Trial he and ten other ANC leaders were sentenced to life imprisonment for political offences, including sabotage.

Nelson Mandela was imprisoned for twenty-seven years, eighteen of which were spent on Robben Island. But although his voice was silenced and not even his picture could be published in South Africa, he became the face of resistance to apartheid. Both local and international communities put increasing pressure on the regime to release him.

Those non-violent pressures eventually led Frederick Willem de Klerk to announce his release in February 1990. At the same time, "De Klerk unbanned the ANC, removed restrictions on political groups and suspended executions." Mandela became a free man at last and unashamedly went back to his former party, the ANC. In 1991, he was elected President of the ANC.

Over the years, Mandela had learnt that armed struggle and violent protest do not lead to a solution to violence. So he used his new position to negotiate with President F. W. de Klerk with a view to having the country's first multiracial elections. But there were many challenges, not least that while "white South Africans were willing to share power … many black South Africans wanted a complete transfer of power."

---

[26] "Nelson Mandela," Biography.com, http://www.biography.com/people/nelson-mandela9397017, p. 3.

As a result, "the negotiations were often strained and news of violent eruptions, including the assassinations of ANC leader Chris Hani, continued throughout the country."[27] Yet Mandela was able to "keep a delicate balance of political pressure and intense negotiation amid the demonstrations and armed resistance."

Negotiation and not violence "prevailed ... and on April 27, 1994, South Africa held its first democratic elections. At age 77, Nelson Mandela was inaugurated as the country's black president on May 10, 1994, with de Klerk as his first deputy."

There were many who urged the new President of South Africa to retaliate for what had been done to him and his people. But because he had learnt that violence begets violence, he instead established the Truth and Reconciliation Commission, which led to public confession of sins against humanity, forgiveness and much reconciliation.

At the same time, he worked hard to protect South Africa's economy from collapse and officially launched South Africa's government economic scheme. For example, "through his Reconstruction and Development Plan, he had the government funding the creation of jobs, housing, and basic health care. In 1996, he signed into law the new South African constitution, which established a strong central government based on majority rule and guaranteed the rights of minorities and freedom of expression."[28]

His life demonstrates that those who trust in a non-violent response to violence will never be put to lasting shame.

The God of Surprises

God's ways are always mysterious and unexpected. We see this in Scripture, where God surprised Paul by not granting him relief when he prayed for it. Paul had healed others, but he prayed three times for his own healing and was told, "My grace is sufficient for you, for my power is made perfect in weakness" (2 Cor 12:9).

---

[27] "Nelson Mandela," Biography.com, p. 3.
[28] "Nelson Mandela," Biography.com, p. 4.

God surprised Moses and Aaron. They obeyed him and went to Egypt, but became frustrated by the fact that all their efforts only resulted in the Israelites enduring more harsh treatment than ever before. Only then did the Lord say to Moses, "Now you will see what I will do to Pharaoh: Because of my mighty hand he will let them go; because of my mighty hand he will drive them out of this country" (Exod 6:1).

He surprised Peter by refusing to allow him to resort to violence. When he thought they were wrongly arresting Jesus and drew his sword to "protect" his master Jesus immediately stopped him, saying, "'No more of this!' And he touched the man's ear and healed him" (Luke 22:50–5).

God surprises us by refusing to allow us to resort to violence. He surprises us even more by using the non-Christians we have just read about to teach Christians how to apply the teaching of their Lord and Master and practise non-violent resistance. He surprises us when we see what they achieved!

In an era of persecution, God is always at work behind the scenes in ways that defy our human imagination. We have faith in this, and live with the assurance that the present violence in Africa will end. The early church, and indeed all past generations of Christians, are a cloud of witnesses of how God has used earlier times of persecution for his glory. He still does this today. There are former Muslims who testify that it was the Christians' refusal to retaliate for the violence done to them that eventually drew them to Christ.[29]

Persecution does not destroy the church but sin does. It is only when Christians in Africa and elsewhere who face grinding poverty and persecution realize this that they will stop being afraid or thinking that the church will be annihilated. The early church absorbed the impact of all forms of persecution and survived and thrived. So in the face of persecution, we must continue to live by kingdom values.

---

[29] Ephraim Kadala, *Turn the Other Cheek: A Christian Dilemma* (Jos, ACTS, 2013).

Study Questions

1. Do some research to learn more about Ghandi and his creative use of non-violence. Is there anything in his method that you can use in your context?
2. Dr Martin Luther King gave a famous speech called "I have a dream" in which he outlined his vision for the USA. What is your vision for your own country? What are you doing to make that vision come true?
3. If you were in Nelson Mandela's place, would you have argued for revenge on those who had oppressed you?
4. Have you ever been surprised by the way God has worked in your life or in the life of someone you know?

15

LIVING BY KINGDOM VALUES

The church has two tasks in the world: proclamation and engagement. We are to proclaim the gospel of salvation and to be engaged in transforming our world by working to bring in the kingdom of God in our community. This entails opening the eyes of the blind, who can see no option other than violence, through embarking on ministry characterized by humility, repentance, forgiveness, reconciliation, justice, love and peace-making. Those are general terms, which is exactly how it should be. No two situations are identical, and so we will need to respond differently in each situation. But in all cases, our response should be compatible with the kingdom values of humility, repentance, forgiveness, reconciliation, justice, love and peace-making.

Humility

Jesus acknowledged the existence of a political culture that makes elites think that they have a divine birthright to rule and to exclude others from political and economic participation in the community. He saw this all around him, and spoke of rulers who enjoy lording it over their subordinates (Matt 20:25) and who impose heavy burdens without lifting a finger to help those they oppress (Luke 11:46). We see the same type of thing happening in northern Nigeria, where elites who were threatened by the presence of Christians and their growing numbers now systematically exclude them from schools and from jobs. Unfortunately, we sometimes see the same thing happening in reverse in southern Nigeria, where Muslims are excluded from opportunities.

Similar situations exist in the rest of Africa too, where Tutsis discriminate against Hutus, Zulus discriminate against Xhosas, and so on. But listen to Jesus' words:

> Not so with you. Instead, whoever wants to become great among you must be your servant and whoever wants to be first must be your slave – just as the Son of Man did not come to be served, but to serve, and to give his life as a ransom for many. (Matt 20:26–28)

As followers of Christ, we must not be self-righteous or behave like those Muslims who see all non-Muslims as infidels and who are thus boastful, arrogant and proud of whom they are before God. They rarely see themselves as sinners. Such an attitude is dangerous, for Christ warned us that "all those who exalt themselves will be humbled, and those who humble themselves will be exalted" (Luke 18:14).

In the kingdom of God, humility reigns. God himself has set the example by making Christians dignified participants and collaborators in his earthly reign of love, justice, and peace. We have no right to this status, for we were all once trapped in trespasses and sins, yet we are now beneficiaries of Christ's resurrection and of God's grace and tender mercy. We should share what we have received with others by treating them with the same dignity that God has treated us. They too are made in his image.

Repentance

Because we are called to humility, our goal must not be to humiliate our enemies or our Muslim neighbours but to help free them from their captivity to sin and violence. One of the clearest ways to signal our humility is to acknowledge any ways in which our own sins and failings have contributed to the current violence.

The trouble with many of us Christians is that we tend to assume that we are the innocent party. We believe we are the ones who have been sinned against. In other words, we feel that we are not the problem; the Muslims are. We are only passive receivers of the harm perpetrated by Muslims. That assumption hinders deeper reflection on the way forward.

We need to start accepting some responsibility for what is happening and repent of our own failure to listen to Christ's call to radical discipleship.

The theme of repentance as a response to violence can be gleaned from two biblical narratives in the Gospel of Luke (Luke 13:1–5).[30] Jesus arrived in Jerusalem after a long day of ministry and came across a crowd talking current events. They were discussing two stories in particular: The first was the murder of Jewish worshippers by Pontius Pilate, or as the story says graphically, the "mingling of their blood with that of their sacrifices". The second was the death of eighteen people who were crushed by a collapsing tower. The news was thus about both a human-caused and a natural disaster.

In those days, it was assumed that violent deaths were the result of violent lives: The worse the sinner, the worse the death. People still make this assumption today, and it is leading them to use the imprecatory prayers. Jesus, however, used the news as an opportunity to issue a sharp warning to the crowd: "Do you think these Galileans were worse sinners than all other Galileans because they suffered this way? I tell you, no! But unless you repent, you too will all perish."

His words remind us that violence should not move us to condemnation of the victims or the perpetrators, but to self-examination. We need to confront our own imperfections and the evil we harbour within ourselves, both as individuals and as communities. We have to ask ourselves: "How are we complicit? How do we participate in systems that allow violence to flourish?" "Do I stereotype others?" "Do I speak of Muslims as 'vipers' or 'cockroaches'?" "Do I celebrate when a mosque is burnt or a Muslim-owned business is burnt, just as Muslims celebrate when a church or Christian-owned business is burnt?" "Do I mourn the death of a Muslim like Adamu, who was in a Christian area when he was told to call his wife and say goodbye, before being ruthlessly killed?" If we have ever been complicit in such actions or failed to condemn them, we must repent or face God's judgement. Our God is not a respecter of persons.

Repentance is the willingness to see our own spiritual and physical nakedness and to turn and face God, the ultimate reality, asking him to

---

[30] In this section, I am drawing on marthame.wordpress.com/2011/09/11/what-is-the-christian-response-to-violence-reflections-for-an-interfaith-panel/

shine his light on that which is shrouded in darkness. It is painful, but it is restorative.

Forgiveness

Once we have recognized our own failings, we will also find it easier to see the perpetrators of violence as being like us in that they too are human beings, who have fallen into sin. This insight will help us to deal gently with the ignorant and those who go astray, because we too are prone to similar weaknesses. They are not uniquely evil and we are not uniquely good.

This insight will also help us come to the place where we can extend forgiveness to them. Such forgiveness is rooted in the acknowledgement that God has forgiven us, and as his children we must act like he does. This was the point that Jesus made when he told the parable about the Unmerciful Servant who refused to forgive another's debts, despite having been forgiven a large debt himself. That servant ended up having to face his master's anger. Jesus ended that parable with the warning, "This is how my heavenly Father will treat each of you unless you forgive your brother or sister from your heart" (Matt 18:21–35).

Forgiveness is not easy. How could it be easy to forgive someone who has killed your husband, your wife, or your child, or destroyed a house or a church you have spent years building? How can you forgive someone who denies you an opportunity for education or a job? We need God's help to do this. That is one reason why we need to keep praying the Lord's Prayer. "Forgive us our debts, as we also have forgiven our debtors" (Matt 6:12). We may forgive someone one day, but feel the old hatred welling up anew when something happens to remind us of our loss. Only through Christ and the indwelling of the Holy Spirit can we have the power to forgive that marks us as those who seek to live as citizens of the kingdom of God.

Reconciliation

If we refuse to forgive, we will seek revenge on those who have harmed us and so perpetuate the cycle of violence. But if we have truly forgiven them, we will not merely stop seeking revenge, we will actively reach out to them to seek reconciliation. This is what Rev. Sunday Gomna did when he not only refused to attack those who had attacked his church but instead sought to reach them by founding a medical clinic. It is what Rev. Yakubu Pam did when he overcame the hatred of Muslims that had made him refuse even to meet with them and became chairman of the Plateau State Inter-Religious Committee, where he developed close relationships with Muslims.

Desmond Tutu, too, knows something about reconciliation, for he was the chairman of South Africa's Truth and Reconciliation Commission that investigated the atrocities committed in South Africa in the apartheid era. He has said that where there is no forgiveness and no willingness to reconcile, there is no future. How can all of us, Christians, Muslims and African Traditionalists, survive if we are not willing to live together with all our regional, cultural, political and religious diversity?

As Christians, we should all know something about reconciliation because we have experienced divine forgiveness and reconciliation with God. Look at what Paul has to say on this subject:

> Since, then, we know what it is to fear the Lord, we try to persuade others ... because we are convinced that one died for all, and therefore all died. And he died for all, that those who live should no longer live for themselves but for him who died for them and was raised again ... All this is from God, who reconciled us to himself through Christ and gave us the ministry of reconciliation. We are therefore Christ's ambassadors, as though God were making his appeal through us. We implore you on Christ's behalf: Be reconciled to God. (2 Cor 5:11–20)

Paul saw himself and his co-workers as ambassadors begging people to be reconciled with God and so enjoy God's love and peace. But when we accept this offer, this reconciliation is not just for our own benefit. God has enabled us to be reconciled to him so that we in turn can become agents of reconciliation, working to bring individuals and groups together. The type of community Paul wants to see among Christians is one "which not only celebrates the achievement of reconciliation and enjoys peace with God having responded to the gospel, but which is also now committed to announcing and embodying the message of reconciliation to the wider world."[31]

In the spirit of a community of reconciliation and transformation, the Christian response to violence may be to offer food to the perpetrators. The Bible says, "If your enemy is hungry, feed him, if he is thirsty, give him something to drink" (Rom 12:20). If I ask God to kill my enemies or I kill them myself, who is left for me to feed? The Bible also says, "Bless those who persecute you" (Rom 12:14) – but if I take revenge, who is left for me to bless? Who can I then urge to "be reconciled to God"?

The imprecatory prayers that Christians in Nigeria and elsewhere in Africa are fond of using are the complete opposite of what we are called to do. When we attack Muslim homes and burn mosques, we should not be surprised that the world accuses Christians of behaving in a way that brings shame to God's name. Instead, we should take the radical step of reaching out to our cousins – the Muslims – believing that peace is achievable and that they too will search for it and work to maintain it. After all, they too are suffering, both at the hands of Muslim extremists and Christian militias.

We must leave revenge in God's hand, as he instructs us, and instead of being overcome by evil, we must "overcome evil with good" (Rom 12:17–21). We must not want our enemies to die but to live and have the opportunity to be reconciled to God.

Justice

Some will respond to what I have said by asking "But what about justice?" If I forgive someone or some group and reconcile with them, how does that serve the justice of God? After all, the Bible clearly teaches that God hates all forms of injustice (Deut 6:19–20). But the same God

---

[31] Peter Rowan, *Proclaiming the Peacemaker* (Oxford: Regnum, 2012), p. 32.

also tells us not to seek revenge for injuries we suffer. The law of Moses contains these words: "Do not seek revenge or bear a grudge against anyone among your people, but love your neighbour as yourself" (Lev 19:18). This verse is so important that Paul quotes it in Romans 12:19: "Do not take revenge, my dear friends, but leave room for God's wrath, for it is written: 'It is mine to avenge; I will repay,' says the Lord." We can leave it to God to deal with those who have abused us.

But leaving revenge to God does not mean that we passively tolerate injustice. God ordered the judges in Israel to judge justly, and his prophets pronounced his judgement on those who act unjustly: "Woe to him who builds his house by unjust gain, setting his nest on high to escape the clutches of ruin" (Hab 2:9). So we too must speak out publicly whenever we see injustice. We must not be hypocrites, who tolerate injustice when it favours our group and condemn it when it favours another one. This was a lesson the Rev. Pam learnt as he chaired the Plateau State Inter-Religious Committee. He recognized that as chairman he had to be unbiased, and listen to and learn from the Muslims as well as the Christians on the committee.[32]

We must also learn to recognize the masks behind which injustice hides. We must courageously expose the self-interest of those who urge us on to violence. Christians must join with Muslims to fight a common enemy: the people who pervert justice through authoritarian regimes and structures that reduce human potential to less than nothing; people whose self-interest and will to power cause them to use innocent citizens as pawns to achieve their political intentions. It is in the interests of those in power to divide us and make us fight each other rather than confront injustice.

Christian and Muslim should thus stop focusing on their religion as a thing that divides them, and instead take a stand upon their human rights and their rights as citizens. We must not passively accept injustice but must strategize how to act in ways that will progressively reduce the possibility of politicians taking advantage of citizens' vulnerability to their political agenda.

In sum, competition for the control of economic and political powers pits Africans against each other. As a result, the ethnic groups in most

---

[32] Pam and Korb, *Fighting for Peace,* p. 20.

African countries are alienated from each other so that it is no longer news to say that many African countries live in darkness and in the shadow of death. When historians write our history, they may say, "In those days Africa had no security; everyone did as he saw fit."

Love

God is a God of justice, but he is also a God of love who cares about human suffering. He showed his love by sending his Son to die for us so that we could be adopted into God's family. He did this even before we knew him, for "while we were still sinners, Christ died for us" (Rom 5:8).

We are called to be like Christ, and so we too must be concerned for those who are suffering. Paul goes so far as to say that love is like a debt that we owe to others and can never pay off (Rom 13:8). We owe love to the Muslims even when they terrorize us or despise us!

How can I possibly say that? It is rooted in Jesus' own teaching in the parable of the Good Samaritan. We know from ancient historians that the relations between Jews and Samaritans were often marked by violence. Even James and John, two of Jesus' disciples, wanted him to call down "Holy Ghost fire" on a Samaritan village. Does the description of that incident sound like anything we experience?

> Jesus … sent messengers on ahead, who went into a Samaritan village to get things ready for him; but the people there did not welcome him, because he was heading for Jerusalem. When the disciples James and John saw this, they asked, "Lord, do you want us to call fire down from heaven to destroy them?" But Jesus turned and rebuked them. Then he and his disciples went to another village. (Luke 9:51–56)

Jesus, who had been rejected by the Samaritans, made a Samaritan the hero of his parable! More than that, he used the example of the Good Samaritan to answer the question, "Who is my neighbour", which itself was sparked by the statement that we are to love our neighbours as ourselves (Luke 10:25–37). We are to be neighbours not only to those who are like us but to anyone who is in need. As Paul reminds us in Romans 13:9–10, we show love for our neighbour by living in accord with the Ten Commandments (not lying or committing adultery, theft, murder, and so on, all of which would harm our neighbour).

You may be surprised to realize that another practical way in which we demonstrate our love or our neighbours is by paying our taxes. The money collected can be used by the government to provide clean drinking water, pay for the construction of roads, and fund things like clinics, schools and hospitals. So when we pay our taxes, we are working for the well-being of society and indirectly promoting conscientious citizenship and good governance. If our taxes are misappropriated, we have a right to speak out and engage in non-violent protest, just as we would speak out against any injustice, but we should not take it upon ourselves to refuse to pay legally required taxes.

Nor should we ignore politics. We need to be informed about what is happening and take an active role in our community in order to do good to our neighbours.

In Matthew 25:31–46, Jesus explains that at the last judgement God will note who has fed the hungry, given water to the thirsty, welcomed strangers, cared for the poor and the ill, and even visited those in prison. In light of this, I was glad to have the privilege of helping distribute relief materials to traumatized Muslim families during the Jos crisis of 2010. At first, they did not want to talk to us. They asked us what Christians were doing there since Christians did not want any Muslims to live in the Plateau State. I could understand their feelings. Several of the women had seen their husbands killed by Christians. One had lost her husband and five children. A Muslim farmer who had borrowed two million naira (more than $1000) to plant a commercial crop was going to lose it all because he was now too afraid to return to his farm.

I explained that we had come to the camp because as Christians we cared about their plight. We recognized their humanity. The same God who created us has also created them. God cares for them, and so do Christians.

Once we had listened to their stories and established rapport with them, they were willing to listen to us. I spent some time talking to a small group about justice, and pointed to the role of political elites in fuelling crises. The group agreed that rich Muslims do not lose their children, wives, husbands, brothers, sisters and parents; nor are their homes and crops destroyed. The rich sit safe while the poor seek refuge in refugee camps. The poor lose everything while the rich lose nothing.

There was little I could do for these people. Our limited relief supplies would never recompense them for what they had lost. But at least in love I could weep with them, try to work with them to understand what was happening, and vow to devote a large part of my life to working to prevent such violence.

Peace-making

Some religious people tend to think that violence is the fruit of righteousness. But that is not what Jesus taught. In his Sermon on the Mount, he declared that peacemakers are blessed and "will be called children of God" (Matt 5:9). One of the ways to know we are using God's wisdom in handling the matter of violence is when our effort results in a harvest of righteousness, for James categorically states, "Peacemakers who sow in peace raise a harvest of righteousness"(Jas 3:18).

May we be able to pray the great prayer of St Francis of Assisi:

> Lord, make me an instrument of your peace. Where there is hatred, let me sow love; Where there is injury, pardon; Where there is doubt, faith; Where there is despair, hope; Where there is darkness, light; Where there is sadness joy.
>
> O Divine Master, grant that I may not so much seek to be consoled, as to console; To be understood, as to understanding; To be love as to love.
>
> For it is in giving that we receive, it is pardoning that we are pardoned, and it is in dying that we are born to eternal life

Study Questions

1. Each day this week, focus on a different aspect of God's kingdom. Write down where you see signs of the presence or absence of kingdom values in others or in yourself. Then share your observations with others.

16

CONCLUSION

"We have no more cheeks to turn" is a cry of desperation. I know only too well the emotions that give rise to such a cry. There is nothing wrong with feeling such emotions. But what is wrong is to give in to the temptation to abandon our commitment to peace and resort to violence. This book is meant to encourage you to stand firm despite the storm around you.

In this book I have given many examples of people who used what they have to work for peace in desperate situations. Yet in telling these stories I have not mentioned the main resource they all share, a resource that is available to the entire body of Christ – prayer. This resource is so important that the apostles regarded it as central to their life and ministry, insisting that "we will give our attention to prayer and the ministry of the word" (Acts 6:3).

Prayer helps us to realize that Christ is the point of convergence we all long for. Prayer is the only way we can ever meet God's demand: "The righteous person will live by his faithfulness" (Hab 2:4b). We cannot please God if we do not have faith in him. Therefore, in order to be found pleasing to God, Paul says you need to "devote yourselves to prayer, being watchful and thankful" (Col 4:2).

The Bible includes the prayers of people who were persecuted and desperate. One of them was Hannah, who was part of a polygamous family and was persecuted by her husband's other wife (1 Sam 1). In a culture where having children is of the utmost importance, being barren is hell on earth. I have seen this myself, for my own mother used to taunt a neighbour's daughter who was barren, driving her almost to the point of suicide. Day after day, year after year, Hannah was teased, taunted, mocked and ridiculed. She would end up weeping so much that she could not eat (1 Sam 1:3–7). Surely Hannah had no more cheeks to turn.

Yet Hannah did not violently attack her tormentor. Instead, she went to the tabernacle to pray. She brought her deep anguish and desperation to the Lord, who rules the universe. And he heard and answered her prayer. More than that, Samuel, the son God granted her, would be the one to usher in a new day in Israel's history, restoring the priesthood and bringing the nation back to God.

Hannah's story shows what faith does. She did not deny her sorrow or her barrenness, but she did not see them as a final verdict. Instead, she brought them to the Lord. We too must take the bull by the horns. There is no need to deny our own heartache and fear. We must not simply praise God and deny the reality before us, turning a blind eye to the horrific conflict in Nigeria. We must bring these things to him, with confident trust in

> his incomparably great power for us who believe. That power is like the working of his mighty strength, which he exerted in Christ when he raised him from the dead and seated him at his right hand in the heavenly realms, far above all rule and authority, power and dominion, and every title that can be given, not only in the present age but also in the one to come. (Eph 1:19–21)

Despite the violence around us, we must not give up on God and his revealed ways. We should cry out like Hannah, and like the prophet Habakkuk we can ask,

> How long, LORD, must I call for help,
> but you do not listen?
> Or cry out to you, "Violence!"
> but you do not save?
> Why do you make me look at injustice?
> Why do you tolerate wrongdoing?
> Destruction and violence are before me;
> there is strife, and conflict abounds. (Hab 1:2–3)

Habakkuk wanted God to do something dramatic to show the world that he hates violence, but that was not the way God was going to operate. So God explained the lesson he wanted people to learn in such situations – perseverance:

> The revelation awaits an appointed time;
> it speaks of the end
> and will not prove false.
> *Though it linger, wait for it;*
> it will certainly come
> and will not delay.

> See, the enemy is puffed up;
> his desires are not upright –
> *but the righteous person will live by his faithfulness.* (Hab
>   2:3–4)

Habakkuk had to be patient and wait for God's own timing, which is always the best. Like him, we must learn to live by faith – that is, to live with confident trust in the Lord our God.

Let me end with one final example of a church that is living by faith in the city of Kaduna, a place that has been rocked by violent conflict between Christians and Muslims. The Christians there have first-hand experience of desperation. In that city, a pastor and his congregation have been fervent in prayer and seeking God's face. They committed themselves to paying careful attention to Jesus' teaching on non-violence and realized that the grace of God, when understood in all its truth, delivers from all forms of desperation. Their confident trust in the glorious power of God has enabled them to demonstrate tremendous faith, endurance and patience.

The church began to reach out to its Muslim neighbours. To demonstrate the unconditional love of Christ to those who did not love them, they started providing assistance to Muslim street beggars and the physically challenged from the Muslim community. They began to hold what they called "Friends' Special Day", a day on which church members invited their Muslim neighbours to the church for a luncheon or dinner. Over time, prominent Muslim and Christian leaders had lunch together and exchanged gifts. Eventually, these leaders promised to work together for peaceful coexistence and the development of their communities.

As a result of the church's willingness to extend a hand of fellowship to the Muslim community, the Muslims have reciprocated by protecting the church whenever there is a conflict in Kaduna.[33]

Like the members of that church, we should be seeking reconciliation rather than revenge. We should be telling stories of hope, rather than stories that promote hatred. We should all be working to ensure that everyone is treated with dignity and given the opportunity to participate fully in the political and economic life of our nation. We should be demanding that our leaders act with integrity and credibility and work for order, justice and peace. We should be working creatively to bring peace by pursuing prayer, love, forgiveness, justice and reconciliation.

We are to follow Jesus, who suffered for others. Think of his life. He knew what it was like to receive messages that others were planning to destroy him (Luke 13:31). He can understand our fear when we receive a text in the night warning us that Muslims are planning an attack. But he did not respond by arming his followers. Instead, he sometimes slipped away to avoid danger, and at other times he openly challenged those who sought to kill him and showed the flaws in their thinking using logical argument and creative parables. He defended the oppressed and cared for the needy. When, in God's timing, his enemies seized him and were apparently triumphant, he still loved them and prayed for God's mercy on them, recognizing that they acted in ignorance. The martyr Stephen followed in his footsteps.

Remember what Scriptures says:

> No temptation has overtaken you except what is common to mankind. And God is faithful; he will not let you be tempted beyond what you can bear. But when you are tempted, he will also provide a way out so that you can endure it. (1 Cor 10:13)

We need to listen to Peter's words to a persecuted church: "Humble yourself under his mighty hand, that he may exalt you in due time; cast all of your care upon him, for he cares for you" (1 Pet 5:6–7).

---

[33]   www.dailytrust.com.ng/daily/indexphp/news-menu/news/21517-christians-muslims-hold-fellowship-dine-together

The God who spoke and the world came into being is faithful. His lovingkindness surrounds us (Ps 32:10), supports us (Ps 94:18), preserves us (Ps 19:88), protects us (Ps 40:11), abounds toward us (Ps 86:5), comforts us (Ps 199:76), revives us (Ps 119:88), and follows us all the days of our lives (Ps 23:6).

Because of his incomparably great power for us who believe, he is able to transform our situation of desperation and agitation into a situation of hope!

APPENDIX 1

CHRISTIAN RESPONSE TO VIOLENCE: AN EMERGING THEOLOGICAL PARADIGM?

The following article by the Revd Gideon Para-Mallam, IFES Regional Secretary for English- and Portuguese-speaking Africa (EPSA), first appeared as an editorial in SPAN on 4 July 2015.

As the prayer meeting progressed, all of a sudden, Al-Shabaab terrorist gunmen burst into the classroom where the students were meeting, randomly and recklessly killing innocent students at will. By then, the students had prayed for more than thirty minutes and had formed a prayer circle holding hands in a symbolic prayer of agreement which captured the spirit of Jesus' admonishment: *"Again, I tell you that if two of you on earth agree about anything you ask for, it will be done in heaven. For where two or three come together in my name, there am I with them"* (Matt 18:19–20).

Rachael was one of the survivors but now lies critically ill in the hospital. When we went to visit her early June, she had already spent a little over two months at the Kenyatta National Hospital, Nairobi, Kenya. As she sat up on her hospital bed, obviously with a lot of physical and emotional pains, her agony could only better be imagined. But the smile on her face showed her unmistakable joy at receiving her guests. The torturing pain showed in her strained turns and twists as she struggled to come to terms with what the doctors told her earlier:

she was paralyzed from the waist down. Rachael said the doctors' pronouncement was very devastating to her. "I need encouragement from within," she said. "The real battle for me is within; the inner war to remain strong and trusting in the power of my God ... Please don't forget me here," she whispered through the pain. "Your presence brings much encouragement to me." She rested her head again on the elevated back and headrest of her hospital bed otherwise known as the *couch.*

Rachael Ikonye is one of the survivors of the April 2, 2015 attack on the Kenyan Garissa University College by the Al-Shabaab terrorist group. On that fateful day, the unjustified attack was carried out when twenty-five students had gathered for the daily Morning Glory prayer meeting at 5:00 a.m. Twenty-two of them were killed in cold-blood. When I shared with Rachael the prayer support she was getting from her fellow students in the global IFES family, her joy was evident. Then she said something that will stick with me for a long time: "Please pray not only for my physical condition and healing, but continue to pray that I remain strong inside. I want to trust God in a deep and personal way as I deal with the present health challenge I have been thrown into by this attack." Two weeks later on June 26th when I had long returned to Nigeria, Rachael sent me this SMS message from her hospital bed: "Thanks a lot. Your prayer helped a great deal. I am quite at peace. Cease not to remember me till I mature in faith ...." During that fateful morning of April 2nd, 144 other students did not make it out of their university college hostel alive. Rachael is one of the students whom the Lord miraculously rescued from this attack.

IFES-EPSA has experienced tremendous growth in the midst of adversity. EvaSue, Ethiopia; NIFES, Nigeria; LIFES, Liberia; ICMB, Botswana and FOCUS, Kenya have witnessed significant numerical growth in depth and have seen thousands of students come to faith in Christ in the last four years. Could the constant barrage of terrorist attacks signify the nature of spiritual warfare we must confront – for the long haul? Many students have wondered how best to respond to or handle their present challenges. Christian students in Nigeria have endured the trauma of studying with an uncertain future. Education for many students right now is at risk of death at the hands of Boko Haram, who are waging a religious and ideological war. During my recent visit and interaction with former Garissa students in Kenya, it was clear that pursuing education while in fear of losing one's life is scary. Some students were nearly tempted to forgo education in order to stay alive, but they are slowly regaining confidence and trusting in the God who rules and controls all things.

The prosperity gospel in some ways denies suffering, and now students are struggling to reconcile this teaching with the reality of what the church is going through under intense persecution. The constant frontal attacks on Christians in Nigeria, and particularly Christian students, has led to many asking questions about what should really be the right Christian response to violence and terrorist attacks targeting them. It is common to hear students and Christians in Nigeria saying things like this: "In 1987, we were slapped, and in obedience to Christ's teaching (referencing Matthew 5:39), we turned the right cheek. Then in 1990 we were attacked again, we obeyed the same passage of Scripture and we turned the left check. In the year 2000, we came under another attack (in the wake of the declaration of the Sharia legal system in most northern states of Nigeria) and now we seem to have no more cheeks left to turn."

From 2010 to date, the church in Nigeria has been living with tension because of constant attacks. The sentiments expressed above echo the plight of Christians living in violent circumstances and raise the all-important question of how best to respond to such violence and brutality. The teachings of Christ regarding what our approach should be when persecuted seem clear. However, there are doubts about the meaning of Christ's injunction and about the best approach to the prevailing situation. Should Christians keep turning their cheeks indefinitely or should they fight back at some point?

This is a profound theological question, not only for Christian students to grapple with but for the whole church, which is asking the same question, not just in Nigeria and Kenya, but across Africa. The crisis which has seen Muslims and Christians fighting tooth for tooth in the Central African Republic, for example, brings the tension to the fore and represents an ugly commentary on the state of the church in Africa.

Some other theological questions being asked by Kenyan students are similar to those of students in Nigeria as they grapple with this situation: "Where was God?" "Why would a loving God allow this to happen?" "How could innocent Christian students who met for a prayer meeting be killed in such a gruesome manner?" In the same room: some survived, some died. So students are tempted to ask: "Is God's love sometimes selective?"

In the midst of these questions, there is now a new thinking in some parts of Africa, which is generally referred to as the "Theology of the Third Cheek." This emerging theological paradigm appears to be based on the teaching of Christ that commands believers not to retaliate (Matt 5:39) and nullifies the Old Testament tooth-for-tooth principle (Exod 21:22–25). This Third Cheek Theology is being seriously considered in church circles all over Africa as part of seeking answers to what the Christian response should be in the midst of the persecution at the hands of Muslims and terrorists that is being experienced right now in many parts of the continent. How should the church react under frontal and physical attack?

In truth, persecution comes with the territory of our Christian faith and should not be considered as something alien. Christians need to have the right understanding of and perspective on what persecution and Christian suffering represents. Jesus made it absolutely clear that Christians will be persecuted. The Bible left no room for ambiguity in giving advance warning that Christians would suffer for their faith in this world. Persecution is suffering for the sake of Christ. Suffering because of one's allegiance to Jesus is what all Christians go through in one form or another. However the magnitude of the suffering differs from one believer to another and from one context to another. A Christlike response as exemplified by young men like Joseph, Daniel and his three friends in Babylon, and by Esther in the palace, shows us that it is possible for Christians to even become more effective witnesses through the suffering they are forced to endure.

The Al-Shabaab attack in Kenya brought this to fore, not just among our own students but also among Christians in Kenya. As George Ogalo, the National Director of FOCUS Kenya observed, the same questions which echo from Nigeria are also a reality in Kenya. It took the Lord's intervention and control to soften hearts after the pain of the Garissa University College attack on that fateful April 2nd 2015, Easter eve, when over 144 university students were killed in one day by terrorists. Without doubt, the boldness of students to live as witnesses for Christ remains unchanged. It is also significant to note that the fear factor such terror attacks seek to implant has not worked to deter our students in the long run!

APPENDIX 2

RELIGIOUS TRENDS AND ISSUES IN NIGERIA

This book is for all who are being persecuted, and not only for Nigerians. However, some of the readers may want to know more about Nigeria, and accordingly I have decided to include this appendix with some information about the history of religion in Nigeria.

* * * *

There are three main religious groupings in Nigeria: African Traditional Religions, Islam and Christianity. Of these, only African Traditional Religions are indigenous religions. Both Islam and Christianity are foreign religions.

In the 1960s and early 1970s, Nigerians enjoyed a relatively high degree of religious tolerance. At that time it could be said that "various Christian denominations ranging from Anglican to Roman Catholic, Methodist, Baptist, Seventh Day Adventist and many others coexist peacefully with each other and with the Islamic faith as well as with traditional religions."[34] However, since the 1980s Nigerians have been experiencing not only religious intolerance and hatred but also religious persecution and wanton destruction of lives and property.

---

[34] Federal Ministry of Information, *Perspectives of Nigerian Culture* (Lagos: External Publicity Division, 1985), cited by Ibrahim Gambari in his chapter "The Role of Religion in National Life: Reflections on Recent Experiences in Nigeria" in *Religion and National Integration in Africa: Islam, Christianity, and Politics in the Sudan and Nigeria* edited by John O. Hunwick (Illinois: Northwestern University Press, 1992), p. 85.

Islam was the first foreign religion to enter Nigeria, a fact of which the Muslims are very proud. It came to Nigeria around the ninth century through North Africa, the Kanem-Borno Empire, and later the Hausa states. In the nineteenth century, it spread like wildfire in Nigeria through the jihad led by Shaihu Usman dan Fodio. Today, Islamic culture and the Hausa-Fulani culture are bedfellows. For example, no one in the Hausa-Fulani culture will ever say that rain has caused destruction. Rather, because Allah does no wrong, the rain he created can only do good. This worldview has become part and parcel of the Islamic culture in northern Nigeria.

Christianity came to Nigeria early in the sixteenth century, first through Catholic missionaries who landed on the coast and later through Protestant missionaries as contact between the Europeans and the coastal and southern peoples of Nigerian increased. It can be said that Christianity is "a religion associated with the coming of the Europeans first as explorers, then as traders, later as missionaries, and finally as colonial rulers".[35] Christianity brought modern education and created a Westernized system of commerce, which gave rise to an industrialized and capitalist society. However, Christianity did not grow deep roots in southern Nigerian culture, as Islam did in the North. Many Christians in the south-west and south-east still retain their traditional worldview. It is only in the Middle Belt region that Christianity put down deeper roots, but even there traditional culture still has a subtle sway.

Neither Christianity nor Islam has succeeded in dethroning the natural human tendencies – self-interest and a preoccupation with material gain, domination and power – which often lead to harmful and destructive interpersonal relationships. These tendencies have deeply affected the relationship between Islam and Christianity. In the years since Nigeria became independent, mistrust, assumptions and fear of domination have characterized the relationship between Islam and Christianity. Between the 1980s and the 2000s, thousands of Christians and Muslims have died in inter-religious violence.

Both Muslims and Christians have engaged in the game of numbers, with Muslims eager to assert that they are in the majority. Scholars like Ibrahim Gambari can cite statistics like the following:

---

[35] Gambari, "The Role of Religion in National Life", p. 86.

In terms of geography, Islam accounts for about 70 percent of the population of the old Northern Region and about 20 to 30 percent of the population of the southern regions. It is important to note that Nigeria contains one of the largest Muslim populations outside the Middle East, which explains the interest that Saudi Arabia, Kuwait, Iran, Egypt, and some other countries of the Islamic world have shown toward Nigeria and Muslims there. While Christianity probably has fewer adherents than Islam relative to Nigeria's total population, it is the dominant religion in the southern regions of the country, and there are also very strong Christian minorities in the northern part of Nigeria.[36]

The trouble with statistics like these is that any change in the percentages is interpreted in terms of victory and defeat. If there is any sign that the proportion of Christians in the north is growing, violence erupts and churches are destroyed. Groups like Boko Haram target pastors, church members and church buildings in an attempt to reduce the number of Christians in northern Nigeria, hoping ultimately to expel them completely.

Christians, too, get agitated when statistical claims are made and assert that they are in the majority. They argue that Christianity is the dominant religion in the old south-west and south-east and in the Middle Belt. Even in some regions where Muslims claim to be the majority, this is no longer completely true: "Although most Hausa-Fulani and Kanuri peoples are Muslims, some Hausa-Fulani and minority ethnic groups in the northern part of Nigeria are strong Christians."[37]

Because there has been no accurate census in Nigeria since 1973, it is impossible to make any accurate claims about the exact proportion of Christians and Muslims in various regions of the country. Moreover, both Muslims and Christians could learn a lesson from the history of Old Testament Israel. Whenever the people of Israel started to celebrate their numerical growth and place their confidence in numbers, God took action. For example, during the reign of Jehu "the Lord began

---

[36] Gambari, "The Role of Religion in National Life", p. 86–87.
[37] Ibid., p. 87.

to reduce the size of Israel" (2 Kgs 10:32). If African Christians and Muslims would remember that God reduces the size of a people who depend on their numerical growth, they might desist from using statistics as an excuse to perpetrate atrocities. It might be no bad thing if religion were eliminated as a category in any future census!

Yet it is also over-simplistic to attribute the crises in Nigeria solely to religious factors, and to imply that religion in any form is always destructive, devastating and bloody. Too often, religion is a convenient scapegoat. Or in more modern terms, religion provides a façade for individuals who, having tasted power and enjoyed its benefits, are reluctant to surrender them. There are many in the elite who will use every available means to maintain the status quo. They have succeeded in employing religion as a strategy that works for their advantage; but to the detriment of the majority.

Sometimes, the elite are not so much individuals as a group, often a numerically dominant ethnic group, who use the resources of the state and the economy for their own benefit, and ignore the needs of other groups. They enjoy unobstructed access to jobs, land, education, credit facilities and other highly coveted privileges and sources of wealth, while other groups do not. This is a recipe for frustration and resentment. Denying others access to political and economic power often leads to civil wars, which may be cloaked in a religious guise.

FURTHER READING

Azumah, John. *My Neighbour's Faith: Islam Explained for African Christians.* Jos: HippoBooks / Grand Rapids: Zondervan, 2008.

Kadala, Ephraim. *Turn the Other Cheek: A Christian Dilemma.* Jos: ACTS, 2013.

Kukah, Hassan Matthew. *The Church and the Politics of Social Responsibility.* Ikeja, Lagos: Sovereign Prints, 2007.

Kunhiyop, Waje Samuel. *African Christian Ethics.* Nairobi, Kenya: HippoBooks, 2008.

Mavalla, Ayuba. *Conflict Transformation: Churches in the Face of Structural Violence in Northern Nigeria.* Oxford: Regnum, 2014.

Mulders, Arne. "Summary of the research report 'Crushed but Not Defeated: The Impact of Persistent Violence on the Church in Northern Nigeria'", prepared for Open Doors International, February 2014. Available online.

Paden, N. John. *Faith and Politics in Nigeria: Nigeria as a Pivotal State in the Muslim World.* Washington, D.C.: United States Institute of Peace Press, 2008.

Pam, Yakubu and Katrina A. Korb. *Fighting for Peace: Learning from the Peace Heroes Among Us.* Jos: FAB Educational Books/YACPIF, 2011.

Sider, Ronald. *Nonviolence: The Invincible Weapon.* Dallas: W Pub Group, 1989.

Stassen, Harold Glen. *Living the Sermon on the Mount: A Practical Hope for Grace and Deliverance.* San Francisco: Jossey-Bass, 2006.

Volf, Miroslav. *Free of Charge: Giving and Forgiving in a Culture Stripped of Grace.* Grand Rapids: Zondervan, 2005.

Wink, Walter. *Engaging the Powers: Discernment and Resistance in a World of Domination.* Minneapolis, Minnesota: Fortress Press, 1992.

www.ingramcontent.com/pod-product-compliance
Lightning Source LLC
LaVergne TN
LVHW051248080426
835513LV00016B/1799